Improving Initial Teacher Training?

new roles for teachers, schools and HE

Edited by

Myra McCulloch and Brian Fidler

In association with
The British Educational Management and Administration Society

Published by Longman Information and Reference,
Longman Group Limited, 6th Floor, Westgate House, The High,
Harlow, Essex CM20 1YR, England and Associated Companies
throughout the world.

A catalogue record for this book is available from The British Library

ISBN 0-582-23685-1

Typeset by Fakenham Photosetting Ltd, Fakenham, Norfolk
Printed in Great Britain by Redwood Books, Trowbridge, Wiltshire

Contents

Notes on contributors

Mary Blight is Headteacher of an Avon Nursery School. For the past eighteen months she has combined this role with that of Teacher Fellow at the University of the West of England. Within the Faculty of Education she is a tutor for a PGCE Early Years Group and contributes to Curriculum Early Years Science. Her teaching career over the past fourteen years has been mainly concerned with young children and PGCE students working in a nursery context. She has been involved in various LEA working initiatives including the Early Years, Highscope and the School Development Plan and currently Science in Avon.

Mike Cornish is Head of the Department of Education Studies at the University of Northumbria. During some twenty-five years in teacher education he has had departmental responsibility for English studies, carried major roles within the CNAA, through its Language and Literacy panel, and undergraduate primary training structures, and co-founded the National Association for Primary Teacher Education Conference (NAPTEC).

Julian Elliott is Principal Lecturer in Education at the University of Sunderland. He is leader of the secondary programme of school-based training and has managerial responsibility for education and teaching studies across all age phases. He taught in special and comprehensive schools for several years prior to practising as an LEA educational psychologist. His research interests are in the fields of behaviour management, psycho-educational assessment and theories of motivation.

Brian Fidler is Senior Lecturer in Education Management at the University of Reading. He trained as a physics teacher at the College of S Mark and S John, London, before doing research at the University of Sheffield and teaching at Huddersfield Polytechnic. He helped train teachers for further education there and schoolteachers at Bulmershe College, Reading before specialising in education management. He has contributed to, and helped edit, *Effective Local Management of Schools, Staff Appraisal and Staff Management in*

Schools and Colleges and *The Supply and Recruitment of School Teachers*. He wrote *ELMS Workbook: Planning Your School's Strategy* with Geoff Bowles and John Hart. He is currently treasurer of BEMAS.

Tor Foster is a Lecturer in Education at the University of the West of England. For the past two years she has been Award Leader for the Primary PGCE course. Her research interests focus on teacher education, language issues, equality of opportunities and links with Eastern European countries. Tor has taught in primary and secondary schools and adult education institutions. Prior to joining UWE she spent four years as an advisory teacher for multicultural education in Gloucestershire.

Cathy Gaunt is Professional Tutor and English Co-tutor for the University of Leicester PGCE Secondary Scheme and Head of English and Teacher Training Co-ordinator at Uppingham Community College in Leicestershire. She qualified in 1978 with a degree in English and is presently studying part-time at the University of Leicester School of Education for a higher degree in educational management. She firmly believes that prospective teachers need a sense of vocation and a thorough level of preparation to equip them for entry to their chosen profession.

Alison Hamer is Head of Wingrove Primary, a large inner city school in Newcastle. She has taught for nineteen years across the whole primary range. Her major interests are in the continuous professional development of teachers and the development of the arts within the primary phase of schooling.

Jenny Harrison has been a biology teacher in a Leicestershire Upper School (14–16-year-olds). She is currently a lecturer at the University of Leicester School of Education, with a particular interest in science education and health education and at the time of writing was Link Tutor and Science Tutor in the PGCE Secondary Scheme. She is a member of the Partnership Steering Committee, with a responsibility and interest in the development of a school tutor training programme.

Maurice Holliday has been Deputy Headteacher of Sandhill View School, Sunderland since its conception in 1987. Prior to this he was Deputy Headteacher at the neighbouring Ryhope Comprehensive School. A former Head of Humanities, he maintains a keen interest in geology, environmental studies and outdoor education. Of particular interest, and high on his agenda, is equality of curricular opportunity, and a desire to promote opportunities for children to take greater responsibility for their learning and engage in self-assessment.

Norman D Lock is Lecturer in Mathematics Education in the Department of Science and Technology Education, University of Reading, having taught and been Headteacher in primary schools between 1970 and 1987. His research interests are chiefly concerned with the developing role of schools in the initial phase of teacher education and the consequent changes in the responsibilities of tutors in higher education. Recent publications, with Myra McCulloch, include 'Student Teachers' School Experience: the managerial implications for schools' *Cambridge Journal of Education* Vol 22 No 1 pp.69–77 and 'Mentorship Developments in the Primary Phase of Initial Teacher Education at the University of Reading' *Mentoring: Partnership in Teacher Education* Vol 1 No 3 Spring pp.21–28.

Myra McCulloch is Dean of the Faculty of Education and Community Studies at the University of Reading. She worked as a teacher and Head of Department before moving to research on school experience in initial teacher education for the Council for National Academic Awards. She subsequently worked in initial and in-service teacher education at Bath College of Higher Education and the former Bulmershe College where she was Deputy Principal. Her research interests are in the organisation and management of higher education, particularly teacher education and equal opportunities.

Carol Park is Principal Lecturer in Education at the University of Sunderland. She is leader of Secondary Programmes as well as the 4-year BA (Hons) in Business Education. Carol taught in comprehensive schools for fifteen years prior to acting as TRIST co-ordinator for an LEA. She subsequently joined the University of Sunderland as Field Officer for the National Business Studies Project. Her research interests are in teaching and learning, PSE and business education.

Beatrice Reed is co-ordinator of academic and professional courses in English in Education at the University of Northumbria. Before working at the university she taught across the primary age range in both England and Canada. Her major interests are the teaching of reading and developing of professional development for teachers.

Joan Whitehead is Associate Dean of Programmes at the University of the West of England. She trained as a secondary teacher before becoming involved in the training of teachers in London, Bath and now Bristol. She has been involved in a number of different partnership developments on the Articled Teacher Scheme, and on Secondary and Primary undergraduate and postgraduate courses and has a responsibility for quality assurance procedures. Her research interests include teacher education policy, its development, implementation and consequences for teacher professionalism.

Preface

The debate in 1993–94 about the creation of a Teacher Training Agency in England has aroused fierce controversy. Its creation could mark a watershed in developments in initial teacher training. The Government's intention is that more training of teachers should be carried out in schools—with or without the involvement of higher education institutions. This book examines a crucial aspect of these changes—the extent and nature of current partnerships between schools and HEIs in the initial training of teachers.

This book is a companion book to *The Supply and Recruitment of School Teachers*, also published in association with BEMAS, in 1993. That book examined the predicted need for teachers and alternative sources of supply. A shortage of trained teachers at the end of the 1980s led to a concentration on alternative forms of preparation in addition to conventional teacher training—refresher courses for returning teachers, and articled and licensed teacher schemes. These latter two schemes were used to launch school-based training as a means of opening up new avenues into teaching to meet a severe staffing crisis. The recession in the economy in the late 1980s has temporarily masked supply problems and despite buoyant recruitment into conventional courses, school-based training with minimal involvement of HEIs is now being propounded as a means of improving the quality of ITT.

This book examines the need for partnerships between schools and HEIs in the initial training of teachers and finds that the longer term consequences of not ensuring an active, substantial and coordinated input from both schools and HEIs will be disastrous for the quality of the teaching force. Four case studies from different teacher training institutions educating both primary and secondary teachers by four-year BEds and one-year PGCE courses demonstrate recent trends towards more fully developed partnerships between schools and the institutions.

The implications for both schools and HEIs of greater co-operation and more time spent by student teachers in schools are explored. A number of unresolved issues including finance are discussed.

The book concludes with a plea for a more rational approach by the Government to the improvement of the quality of initial teacher training. There is abundant evidence from the study of conventional courses and the newer articled and licensed teacher schemes to be able to devise worthwhile and workable improvements rather than impose ideological changes with predictable long-term reductions in the quality of trained teachers.

It is in everyone's interest in education to improve the quality of teacher training and development—from initial teacher training through induction into further professional development—but this can only be achieved by a constructive dialogue among knowledge-able contributors.

Myra McCulloch
Brian Fidler
The University of Reading
June 1994

Introduction

The aim of this volume is to represent some of the elements of the current dialogue in the development of partnership schemes of initial teacher training. It also seeks to provide a critical framework within which issues and concepts which have been treated as relatively unproblematic can be re-examined and re-considered.

This book is a companion to *The Supply and Recruitment of School Teachers* (Fidler et al. 1993). Whilst that book examined alternative sources of trained teachers to meet an impending shortage, this book concentrates on changes to mainstream teacher training: the partnership between schools and higher education institutions to educate and train teachers.

The way in which this book is conceived is as a tripartite presentation in which the scene is set and the context established; particular examples of interpretation of policy are examined and general issues emerging from policy are pursued.

Intrinsic to the structure of the book is an understanding of partnership which seeks to give all partners their voice. Many of the schemes being developed currently seem to seek to continue the practice of a somewhat hierarchical relationship where expertise is seen to belong more clearly to one set of participants than another. Our understanding of partnership is one where all participants have a contribution to make which is valued for its particular and distinctive nature. Our interpretation of that view is made explicit in the book through the involvement of teachers as authors of their own partnership experience. As school-based schemes develop it will also become increasingly important to hear the voice of students whose pattern of training will be rather different from what has gone before.

The first two chapters address policy issues in teacher preparation over the past decade (McCulloch) and look specifically at how partnership policies have developed (Fidler). It is important to note that although school-based schemes are developing at a particularly fast rate at the moment in response to the impetus created by government instigated policy change, a number of initial preparation courses had already moved to establish a distinctly school-based ethos. The best known of these is, of course, the Oxford internship Scheme (Benton 1991) but a number of institutions had made such progress that the Department for Education Circular 9/92 (DFE 1992) required less change in structure, aims and content than in the resource base for new courses following the transfer of resource to schools.

The four examples from institutions around the country therefore look both to the origins of their programmes in developing practice and the changes demanded by policy initiatives. All types of courses are covered from one-year primary to four-year secondary and a variety of solutions to the shared problems are offered. Interestingly, several shared themes emerge.

Chapter 3 discusses the Postgraduate Certificate in Education at the University of the West of England (Whitehead, Foster and Blight) in relation to the training of primary teachers. The concern to develop 'an overall model of sound and effective professional practice' which provides both a commitment to reflective practice and the fulfilment of the requirements of the government circulars is one shared by all the authors. Professional characteristics such as autonomy are highlighted and the search for authentic collaboration with a unified perspective on the nature of the task between teachers and tutors is stressed. What we are concerned with is the joint delivery of higher education.

Chapter 4 looks at the PGCE (Secondary) at the University of Leicester. Jenny Harrison and Cathy Gaunt discuss a partnership scheme in which not only teachers and tutors but students, pupils and parents are seen as having a role. The notion of the school in the community confirms a view of there being various sites of learning both formal and informal, all of which contribute and none of which is sufficient. The fear that rapid change accompanied by diminishing resource will undermine the effectiveness of partnership schemes is made explicit; a fear shared by the other authors in this volume.

The third example, Chapter 5 considers the four-year undergraduate course for primary teachers at the University of Northumbria (Cornish, Hamer and Reed). The themes of strong professional ethos, the whole-school context, the notion of reflective practice among teachers, tutors and students and the congruence of work carried out on university and school sites run through this account. The mutual benefits to be gained from partnership are placed in sharp relief when it is argued that current policies actually destabilise the concept of partnership.

Similarly, the account of Sunderland's two- and four-year courses for secondary teachers (Elliott, Park and Holliday) emphasises the existence of established partnerships which had to be revised fundamentally in the light of current policies. The emphasis on preparing a questioning, analytical, reflective practitioner is confirmed and the fear is made explicit that an emphasis on the competences identified in the latest circulars will undermine this and lead, before too long, to the demise of the BEd degree for secondary teachers.

All four accounts show a positive response to the policy constraints and opportunities currently faced by all teacher educators. The third part of the book picks up some of these issues and examines them in detail.

Myra McCulloch (Chapter 7) looks at teacher competences and their assessment, seeking to identify some of the ways in which different definitions of these terms have developed and looking at the implications of these differences for the assessment of a student teacher in respect of Qualified Teacher Status. The difficulties of assessing competence through performance are established and concerns are raised about the ways in which simplistic behaviourist models of competence may add up to something considerably less than the newly qualified teacher we currently aspire to prepare.

Fidler and Lock (Chapter 8) look at both primary and secondary mentorship schemes and locate these in issues of whole-school development. The notion that mentorship can be anything other than a whole-school commitment is challenged and the development of the student as teacher in the context of a school community is firmly established. This chapter confirms the view that new forms of partnership, although rooted in developments over the past ten years are actually necessarily representative of a transformed relationship.

McCulloch (Chapter 9) considers this transformation and identifies problems of the management and implementation of change in respect of partnership not simply in schools but in a parallel yet insufficiently recognised way, in universities. The assumption that all the changes made necessary by partnership are being experienced in the schools is challenged, not simply from the point of view of managing a diminishing resource but also in terms of the nature of the university tutor's role and its transformation within a system where both schools and universities are jointly responsible for delivering higher education.

In the final chapter, Fidler and McCulloch draw together the themes and issues raised in the book and ask, will these changes improve Initial Teacher Training? As with most analyses of processes the response tends to be a rather better set of questions than a series of answers. Inevitably, the need for adequate resources is highlighted but this is alongside the recognition that despite the hostility of the environment, the vulnerability of teacher educators (teachers and tutors) to job loss and the determination of the government to consult with its eyes and ears closed, there are some magnificent experiments continuing to enhance our teacher education provision.

We are most grateful to the contributors to this volume and to our editors at Longmans, Roger Henwood and Nicola Reavley for their encouragement, support and enthusiasm.

Myra McCulloch
Brian Fidler

Part 1
The changing context for teacher education

1 Improving initial teacher training?: Policy in action 1984–1994

Myra McCulloch

Introduction

It is almost inevitable that any book on changes in Initial Teacher Training (ITT) will be written in a context which alters throughout the process of writing and that events have a way of undermining the most evident of trends. Nevertheless it is argued here that there are significant and coherent patterns of policy making which have been made explicit through a series of Department of Education and Science and latterly Department for Education circulars and legislation. These show a clear and developing strategy for ITT which is already implemented in part through the changes in patterns of course provision and delivery in higher education institutions and schools. A profound effect on the structures and practices of ITT throughout the rest of this century will continue to be felt as existing and proposed reforms are made concrete.

This chapter seeks to outline policy developments since 1983 and to identify the implications for planning, implementation and management (including resource management) for institutions of higher education and those schools both in the secondary and primary age phases which have long been and will increasingly be concerned about and involved in Initial Teacher Training. Perhaps one of the first things to discuss is the use of the term 'Training' rather than 'Education' in reference to the initial preparation of teachers. The official signification of initial teacher preparation is that it is Training (hence ITT). The changing emphasis on skills and the practical combined with an under-informed notion of what educational theory is about promotes this choice of designation. For teacher educators the use of education in the title of initial preparation course (hence ITE) signifies the break between short, instrumental courses of training for a sorely needed but undervalued profession and the longer, more reflective periods of higher education offered over the past twenty or so years to student-teachers. Kelly (1993) observes that 'while the kind of critical study of education . . . along with the provision of opportunities for teaching and research . . . fits well with the concept of a university as a centre for free, independent and open exploration of human knowledge and understanding in all spheres, the idea that universities should offer forms of *training* which fall well short of this definition is difficult, indeed impossible, to justify' (p.132). The consultative document 'Education in Schools' (DES 1977) showed a welcome consensus in views between the Secretaries of State and the Education establishment in its advocacy for a high quality, all-graduate profession for whom initial preparation was just that, the beginning of a lifetime commitment to professional development. The emphasis was on the importance of teacher education being integrated within general higher education provision, with a commitment to an all-graduate profession and to research and development which support high quality teaching in our schools. There was also recognition of a gap in the 'current arrangements for the development of the content on teacher education' (p.28) and the commitment to 'discuss with the teachers' and other interested organisations how this gap might best be filled' (p.28). The current agenda for the reform of teacher education serves, sadly, to highlight the enormous difference in the views now held by the political policy makers and those involved in education at all levels who are called upon to implement policy changes about which they feel ambivalent if not antagonistic and which have been formulated with but cursory procedures for consultation. The past ten years, on which this chapter is focused, show not only the singularly determined way in which policy has been directed but also an enormously significant change in whose voices are heard in respect of policy formation.

Broadfoot (1986) describes the administrators in the then Department of Education and Science who have traditionally acted according to '. . . the consensus of tradition and custom, the assumption of control where none exists and the power to manipulate the ingredients of debate which are crucial in determining policy outcomes on English education' (p.56). These ingredients include, for example, the use of democracy and majority voting, recognition of managerial authority and hierarchical responsibility and cognizance of accepted codes of professional practice. What Broadfoot points to, through the 1980s, is the breakdown of the traditional consensus on which the politics of influence were based and the increasing use of explicit power, through the parliamentary system, to make explicit policies which have the force of law. Broadfoot comments, 'It remains to be seen how long HMI, the Examination Boards and other sources of the criteria of professional accountability can continue to resist the covert incursions of the contemporary political climate' (p.61). Clearly, when writing in 1986, she still believed that it was the professionals 'who are the major source of influence on the "normative climate" which is reinforced and disseminated through professional discourse' (p.59). It would be very hard to hold that line in 1994. The proposed transfer (Education Bill 1993) of all funding and related matters in teacher training to a new agency, a quango with a membership directly appointed by the Secretary of State and accountable only to him and of whom only half may be from the world of education is just one indicator of how the policy context has changed. Rather than a consensus in teacher education, there are now, quite clearly, competing cultures engaged in struggle at the levels of policy formation, implementation and review.

A review of policy in teacher education from 1983

The 'failure' of education to respond to the needs of the nation has been a key topic in the political arena since the mid 1970s along with the desire to make more accountable all areas of educational provision. Teaching in Schools; The Content of Initial Training (DES 1983a) was published in 1983 as a consultation document following much informal discussion the previous year about the ways in which teacher education could best be improved. A White Paper followed shortly after (Teaching Quality DES 1983b) and this, in 1984, was made precisely explicit in the publication of Circular 3/84. This circular represented, in some ways, the establishment of a National Curriculum for teacher education. The new vehicle by which accountability was to be both established, monitored and reviewed, nationally and locally, was the Council for the Accreditation of Teacher Education (CATE). This body was to have an advisory role to the relevant Secretaries of State (Education and Science and Wales) in respect of the approval of courses of initial teacher preparation in England and Wales during which process an evaluation would be made of each course in respect of explicit criteria set down by those Secretaries of State. Its founding chairman argued that the establishment of CATE reflected a concern with the content and quality of teacher education which was worldwide (Taylor 1990) and that although teacher educators were relatively used to being criti-

cised, having neither the status nor power of other educational establishments, the difference in the late 1970s and early 1980s was that
the criticism 'was much more sharply focused on the process and
content of teacher education itself, rather than its alleged educational
and social characteristics' (p.112). The criteria employed from 1984
'some aspects of which stimulated lively debate' (p.114) 'deal with
the selection of students, qualifications and experience of staff, organisation of courses, balance of subject studies and subject method,
educational and professional studies, and assessment and certification' (p.114). One of the key lively debates which the criteria
promoted was on the role of subject studies in primary ITE, a debate
still raging in the light of the latest Circular on primary teacher
training, Circular 14/93 (DFE 1993a). Another area where policy has
become increasingly focused was also made explicit in 3/84; that of
the role of schools and the nature of the contribution they are best
able to offer. The circular introduced criteria relating the role of the
training institutions to that of the schools with which they worked
and promoted a view of partnership in which schools would become
increasingly involved, not only in the supervision of students during
their school placements but also in their selection for the course, in
the planning and delivery of the course in the higher education
institution (HEI) and indeed, in assessment. As a corollary to this,
tutors in education departments who were concerned with pedagogy
should be able to show recent, relevant and successful experience
teaching in schools within the age range for which they were preparing student teachers. Publication in 1989 (DES Circular 24/89,
1989b) of revised criteria, required even more recent and relevant
school teaching by tutors and made more explicit the requirements
in respect of particular curricular areas. Again the growing need to
involve serving teachers more comprehensively in the initial preparation process can be traced and we can find in this circular the
beginnings of the identification of competences for acquisition by
students by the end of their course (DES 1989b).

Taylor suggests that the period of the late eighties showed the
effects of CATE in improved standards of teacher preparation. He
refers to *The New Teacher in School* (HMI 1988) and the Report of
the Senior Chief Inspector (SCI) (DES 1989c) which reported on
Standards in Education 1987–88. The improvements included, 'improved balance between theory and practice; a higher proportion of
staff with recent and relevant experience of teaching in schools;
better links between institutional and school-based work; more effective partnerships between institutions and schools; improved academic rigour in courses; a clear subject/curriculum match ...'
(p.121), all reflected in the confident and enthusiastic response of
student teachers. Some weaknesses, it was acknowledged, con-

tinued; Taylor identifies these as 'lack of sufficient preparation in the organisation and management of learning; poor assessment and recording of pupils' progress, an undeveloped understanding of ways in which children learn and develop; and problems in dealing with different levels of ability' (p.121).

These weak areas are specifically identified as necessary competences for teachers in the Circular 9/92 which replaced 24/89 in respect of the secondary age phase and in Circular 14/93 which makes explicit new criteria for the training of primary phase teachers. The most significant aspect of these two latest circulars, however, reflects the coming to fruition of the policy first heralded in 1984; the increased role of schools in the training of teachers. Although partnerships are still seen as important where training is provided by HEIs together with schools and CATE has published extensive advice on how these partnerships can best be developed (CATE 1992) it is now possible for schools to elect to train, either on their own or in consortia, student teachers who need have no contact with higher education during their period of training. The possibility of being awarded Qualified Teacher Status (QTS) without benefit of a higher education course and award was heralded in the Licensed Teacher Scheme introduced in 1990 (DES 1989a) but whilst this scheme promoted an alternative mode of entry into teaching, another policy intention (McCulloch 1993a), it was aimed in particular at members of the community who had teaching qualifications from overseas which did not make them immediately eligible for QTS but which gave them an educational background more like that of teachers in this country. It is a quite new idea for students to be awarded a license to practice without any reference to the institutional quality assurance mechanisms and academic standards established this century within teacher education.

Although it is argued that diversity in routes of entry into teacher education is the aim of this policy and that the traditional higher education route will continue to be substantial in its contribution to the professional education of intending teachers, the potential debasement of professional training must be acknowledged. 'The study of education, properly conceived, has an important role to play in such a system, since it is only through education that democracy can renew itself and develop. Conversely, the de-skilling of the teaching profession must ultimately lead to a de-skilling of society itself' (Kelly 1993 p.138). As is argued later in this volume, the contributions to be made to teacher education by schools and HEIs are distinctive but different and the students' experience is enriched by a process of learning which involves both of these sets of expertise, in partnership. The exclusion of either of these partners must call into question the potential quality of the provision.

It is also interesting that one of the prime justifications for the proposed establishment of the Teacher Training Agency is that it will be able to determine how to share out the various funds available for ITT between School Centred schemes (SCITT) and Partnership schemes. If it is envisaged that SCITT will remain a small(ish) endeavour then it seems rather excessive to establish a new quango to take care of it. Indeed, in Wales it is proposed to handle this through a sub-committee of the main funding council and various bodies in opposition to the current reforms (The Committee of Vice-Chancellors and Principals (CVCP) and the Teacher Alliance for example) have proposed this as a suitable vehicle in the English context. The reluctance of the Government to respond to the almost universal criticism of their proposals suggests that the agenda is not based simply on the explicit.

Implications for the planning of ITT courses

The planning of initial teacher preparation courses has, over the past ten years, always included teacher involvement but it is likely that the extent of such involvement has varied. One can speculate on a number of ways in which teacher views could be sought: planning team membership, where full executive rights are given and full participation is expected; meetings of advisory groups where teachers are invited to comment at various stages of the planning and their views are fed in to the work of the planning groups—a less powerful but still useful role to play; teacher conferences where a large group of teachers, quite often heads, are invited in to be informed of progress and to comment—a much less effective forum from the point of view of teachers but at least allowing input from the profession. Effective communication of planning and development work is probably achieved through a combination of these various strategies. If teachers are invited to be full members of planning teams, they may be representative of the local teaching community but the effectiveness of community involvement will be dependent upon their ability and willingness to consult their constituency; advisory groups are similarly representative but again, communication with the larger community depends on their goodwill and effectiveness; teacher conferences, with the sole aim of dissemination, do reach a high proportion of the schools with whom HEIs work but there is a real problem in making the assumption that involvement of heads (this is particularly pertinent in relation to primary schools where heads are likely to be the only people available during the day (and late meetings create other difficulties)) means that the body of school staff will be informed about the project. Chapter 8 examines the implications for schools of taking a significant part in initial training. In particular it suggests that this should be recognised in each school as a whole-school development needing whole-school discussion and planning. The difficulties for HEIs of ensuring widespread knowledge and understanding of what is involved in every school are regarded as problematic.

Nor is this a criticism. One of the major drawbacks of the current policy initiatives and one which has been emerging gradually since 1984 is the insufficient grasp by policy makers of the different educational purposes embraced by teachers and higher education lecturers. It is certainly true that teachers have a great deal to offer the professional development of beginning teachers but it is equally true that their first consideration is and must always be, the education of the *children* in their care. It is evident that higher education lecturers involved in pedagogy are trained teachers, selected, at least in part, for their role in higher education because of their skill and experience as classroom practitioners. But their first priority is, and must always be, the education of the *student teachers* in their care for the better promotion of enhanced classroom practice. Planning of courses must make explicit and take account in the organisation of teaching and learning the distinctive interests of all parties; only then can mutual interests be served.

The next stage of planning reflects this difference in prime purpose for it suggests the separation of those aspects of student teacher learning which teachers are best placed to provide from those which HEI lecturers are best placed to provide. McIntyre (1993) describes this agenda setting as making '*suggestions for practice in learning how to teach*; and the evaluation of these practices . . . mainly through the discussion of research-based knowledge about teachers' thinking, classroom practice and learning' (p.51). This is best accomplished where there is 'a shared understanding about the nature of the knowledge which it will be useful to develop and about the means by which it may be best be developed' (p.51).

Thus, a process of learning accompanies an identification of the content of teacher education. Discussion, evaluation and reflection are the processes which must be learned and developed in relation to a content which is deemed to be useful by both parts of the partnership.

Nothing so far has been said of location. There can be no simple argument 'to support the presumption that increased school experience will, of itself, improve the overall quality of teaching in schools' (Carr 1993 p.17). There are some activities, some skills, and some knowledge which are best located in schools. Indeed, for classroom practice the school is the most obvious location. However, location should not determine the nature of teaching and learning without reference to more complex factors. HEI tutors have a key role to play in school-based learning and teachers have a clear contribution to make to institution-based teaching. The evaluations of the Articled Teacher Schemes (Stradling et al. 1991; HMI 1991) identify the student perceptions of a lack of sufficient time to reflect on classroom practice away from the pressures of the school day as a key weakness in the scheme. This might well be a university-based activity in which teachers play an important part.

However, it is equally important to recognise that recommendations on the disaggregation of teacher preparation curricula and the strategies embraced for subsequent integration of the overall student experience must recognise the local context as central to the nature of the discussion. It may be possible, by this element of local flavouring, to reintroduce legitimate distinctiveness and difference between courses of initial preparation where all the odds seem in favour of similarity and central control.

The development of planning procedures which take these factors into account will contribute effectively to the maintenance and improvement of academic standards since the nature of the debate between partners cannot take place without problematising educational knowledge—what Kelly (1993 p.138) describes as 'a fearless search for knowledge and understanding . . . untrammelled by political controls'. What begins as training in the views of the policy makers can be transformed into education during implementation. Yet, at the same time, it is becoming evident that the close collaboration and integration of the work of schools and HEIs on these programmes reduces the flexibility and spontaneity of some teaching and learning experiences. Where institution and school-based work are planned in detail to mix and match, the freedom to divert has to be restricted. It is essential, therefore, that planning strategies are accompanied by rigorous monitoring procedures to prevent the ossification of such schemes.

This is also centrally important for the maintenance of standards. The quality assurance mechanisms for these courses must be seen to be impeccable if HEIs are to continue to offer awards for initial teacher preparation. If universities cannot be convinced that quality is being maintained and validation is withdrawn, all hopes of sustaining teacher education in the light of government reforms will be lost and the 'deliberate attempt to de-intellectualize the education of teachers and, thus, the teaching profession' (Kelly 1993 p.134) will have been successfully accomplished.

Implications for the implementation of partnership schemes of teacher education

The notion of partnership is examined in more detail in Chapter 2 of this volume. Chapter 9 takes the issue of implementation in respect, particularly, of the impact of partnership schemes on institutions of higher education. This section will, therefore, simply seek to identify some of the implementation issues likely to be encountered.

The first of these is the establishment of the partnership itself; the engagement with local schools and the agreement of those schools that they will take part in a form of initial preparation about which they have mixed feelings and for which they have no obligation. HEIs must take into partnership any school which so requests, unless a reasoned case can be made for refusal and the Secretary of State could, if the case is seen as inadequate, withdraw the accreditation of that institution for initial teacher training (DFE 1992, 1993a). Schools, on the other hand, have no obligation to take part in ITT and there is some evidence from the implementation of the secondary schemes, that the provision of sufficient schools for these partnerships is extremely problematic.

These problems are exacerbated by the question of payment for school experience. On the one hand, schools object to the notion that only 'additional' work will be paid for. This, based on the argument that existing school budgets cover existing school placement arrangements enrages the most cooperative of headteachers. If there is such money in existing budgets, they ask, why do schools not engaged currently in teacher education get their budget on the basis of the same formula?

On the other hand, the notion that there is a pot of gold from which schools can claim funding for teacher education obscures the fact that the staffing budget in HEIs is virtually the sole location of sufficient funds for transfer. The systematic reduction in staffing in HEIs to accommodate resource transfer affects more than the provision of initial teacher education—in-service and research capacity are significantly affected by the reduction in range of staff expertise and the professionalism of teaching is further undermined.

Effective partnership might again be the transformatory vehicle for the maintenance and enhancement of professional development at all levels. The negotiation of funding transfer calls upon total commitment of all parties to sustain and develop effective courses of initial teacher preparation.

The management of initial teacher training

'... uncertainty is almost all that management can be certain of' (Bennett et al. 1992 p.1). It is clear that the management of ITT is the management of change; that this change takes place within a context where turbulence has been felt for the past several years and where a series of externally imposed changes have been accommodated at great cost to the teaching profession. For example, the accommodation of externally imposed change affects levels of professional autonomy and thus professional esteem. Margaret Archer (1985) suggested that as education is increasingly affected by the external, it becomes increasingly difficult to protect professional and academic values—there is far less control over certification and training, less ability to take positions of educational control, less capacity to propagate 'pure' academic values and increasingly less capacity to promote internal innovation.

Stewart (1991) argues that management is now concerned with far more complex sets of relationships; that a greater vulnerability is felt to the unpredictable externally imposed changes, that a wider range of activities and functions must be performed with reduced resources and increased accountability and more rigorous performance assessment criteria are in use. This description fits the management of ITT extremely well and focuses on the competing strands of the management task. Rigorous self-assessment may be one way forward for effective managers but the development of collegiality throughout the network of relationships involved will probably provide greater and more effective support. This theme will be pursued in Chapter 2 as the partnerships which form the foundation for effective ITE are discussed.

Summary

Initial teacher education is in a period of transition. Externally imposed policy changes are being interpreted by institutions in the light of their local circumstances and a number of experimental approaches can be found, four of which are reviewed in Part 2 of this volume.

Change of this magnitude, particularly where it is incorporated into four-year programmes of study, takes a long time to implement and even longer to evaluate. It is clear, however, that teachers and teacher educators fear that the reforms currently proposed may undermine the quality of initial teacher preparation. Schemes by which the best of the old can be safeguarded and the new brought into being are sought by all those who value an effective initial training for teachers.

The affirmation of partnership between schools and HEIs as the most appropriate and effective way of achieving this does not make the achievement of effective partnership any less problematic. This is discussed in more detail in the next chapter.

2 Partnership in teacher education: partnership, integration and funding implications

Brian Fidler

Introduction

Historically the evolution of teacher preparation in England and Wales has involved both schools and higher education institutions working together. Indeed both have been seen as essential contributors until recently. New forms of training in the shape of the articled teacher scheme and more particularly the licensed teacher scheme (Fidler et al. 1993) devised in the late 1980s attempted to place a greater emphasis on the contribution of schools, if not entirely replacing the role of HEIs. CATE criteria have placed increasing requirements for more school experience during training and Circulars 9/92 for secondary training and 14/93 for primary training have called for a greater role for schools and teachers in the training process. Thus some form of partnership could be taken as necessary either by historical precedent or by recent Government diktat. However, before accepting the need for partnership and, indeed, hoping to clarify the requirements for any partnership in a more fundamental way than either of the two reasons mentioned above, this chapter proposes to spend some time examining the nature of the training process and trying to demonstrate the need for partnerships between higher education and schools.

In addition to a consideration of the training process and what it should encompass, there is a prior question: what is the nature of the activity for which training is being carried out? Although the activity is generally taken to be teaching, there is a further requirement and that is the need to prepare trainees to work in schools. Thus teacher preparation must include:

1. preparation to teach, and

2. preparation to work in schools.

Preparation to teach

Any fundamental discussion of preparing trainees to teach must begin with an examination of the nature of teaching since it can reasonably be assumed that any preparation will be contingent on an assessment of the activity which is to be the outcome of training.

Before looking at teaching in detail, it may be instructive to ask 'what kind of activity is teaching?' Those who have analysed teaching in this way have taken the generic possibilities to include labour, craft, science, art and profession (Mitchell and Kerchner 1983; Darling-Hammond et al. 1983). As will become clear, teaching does not neatly fit into any of these categories and indeed there has been much discussion recently about how the balance of a teacher's work has moved from one category to another particularly since the introduction of a prescriptive National Curriculum in England and Wales.

Teaching as labour

There is general agreement that the job of a teacher has been de-skilled to some extent by the Education Reform Act since much curriculum decision-making has been removed from schools (Walsh 1987). However, to view teaching as labour would imply that teaching had been 'routinised' (Mitchell and Kerchner 1983) and reduced to a few simple rules which a teacher was required to follow. Close supervision would be required to deal with any non-standard cases and to ensure compliance with the rules. In this conception, training would consist of learning simple rules and how to apply them in practice. Although some have likened the emerging teacher's role to this, this is only a grotesque exaggeration. In any case, following the Dearing Review of the National Curriculum (Dearing 1994), more freedom is to be given to teachers and schools to choose up to 20 per cent of pupils' curricular programme.

Teaching as craft

A craft has a set of specialised and skilled physical techniques and any operation is made up of the results of applying the appropriate techniques. The techniques are either used in standard combinations or are varied for a particular commission. The craftsperson would be expected to be able to envisage the results of applying any particular technique and advise accordingly. The oversight required would consist of agreeing with the craftsperson the nature of the techniques appropriate for a particular case. This would be done by judgement and knowledge of previous practice rather than by theoretical knowledge. Training would consist of working alongside and under the tuition of a highly skilled craftsperson and learning 'by doing'.

Teaching as science

If teaching were a science there would be theories of human learning and behaviour which had been tested in a systematic way. The teacher's job would be to apply these theories whilst keeping records of cases where they did not work as planned so that these cases could be investigated further in order to produce better theories. All theories would be regarded as provisional. The supervision required would be to note exceptions so that these could be investigated and better more comprehensive theories constructed. Training would have a large theoretical component. This would cover learning the scientific method of teaching and of investigation and acquiring knowledge and understanding of the range of theories currently known followed by working as a junior member of a team under guidance. In-service training would be required for updating on new techniques and theories. Whilst teaching as a science may be difficult to justify, Gage (1978) has argued that there is a developing scientific basis for teaching. Although he admits that this is only ever likely to be probalistic rather than deterministic and that teachers will require an art to use this scientific basis.

Teaching as art

Although teaching as a practical art would have some standard techniques, the art of the teacher would be to assemble these and apply them in new and unconventional ways. The act of teaching would be a performance—different every time. Supervision would consist of grading and judging each performance offering advice on techniques but recognising that it is results which count even if achieved through unconventional means but the judgement would be based on aesthetic rather than practical grounds. Training would require learning of techniques but this would be supplemented by experimentation in their use and learning from watching a variety of other skilled performers in order to acquire a repertoire of experiences and ideas. Any theories would be intensely personal ones.

Teaching as a profession

A profession has some elements of a craft (learning by doing), an art (different individuals respond to similar situations in different ways at different times) and a science (there are underlying principles of child development and learning, for example). In addition there are certain requirements which have generally been associated with the high status and older professions. A profession has a specialised vocabulary. It has theoretical knowledge. There is a long period of training and tutelage which has to be successfully completed. A profession has a set of standards which are enforced by a corporate body of peers (Johnson 1972). The professional tailors theoretical knowledge and standardised procedures to the needs of the individual client.

As Dinham and Stritter (1986) observe:

> Reliance on theory is among the most telling distinctions
> between a profession and a trade or craft (p.952).

Training for professionals generally has a theoretical content which is acquired in higher education and also a period of tutelage within a professional setting. Although there are a number of different models in different professions, the entitlement to practice as a professional is granted by the professional body and not by higher education institutions although a degree from a higher education institution may have been a prerequisite.

Jarvis (1983) claims that a significant aim of professional education in addition to the acquisition of appropriate knowledge is the acquisition of a professional ideology:

> that ideology is about the desire to continue to learn in order to
> be the master of the professional knowledge upon which the
> practice is founded, so that the practitioner can render the best
> service to his clients (p.51).

Preparation to work in schools

In addition to the skills of teaching, the preparation of teachers needs to take account of the working situation of the teacher. Working in schools involves working co-operatively with other teachers, teaching support staff, external support staff, parents and governors. It involves an understanding of how schools function.

Here also knowledge and understanding of school organisation is required before appropriate preparation for working in schools can be devised. There have been a number of attempts to describe and analyse how schools work. Each offering takes one particular facet of the school thus each is incomplete but together they offer a number of dimensions on which to model differences between schools.

The dimensions which will be mentioned here include:

(a) leadership style

(b) decision making

(c) organisational structure.

Although these are related and certain combinations on each of these three dimensions would represent a particularly consistent set of values, in practice schools can be found with many combinations.

(a) leadership style

The leadership style of the headteacher and other managers within the school will be highly influential. Both theoretical and empirical studies have examined the leadership style of primary and secondary headteachers. These range from the autocrat to the participative team leader.

A concern in professionally staffed organisations is the tension between the head teacher as 'leading professional' and as 'chief executive' (Hughes 1985). As more managerial functions have been delegated to the headteacher and governors following the Education Reform Act (Fidler 1989a) a tendency has been identified for the headteacher's function to be seen as the manager of other managers or chief executive. In the past, studies of headteachers have identified a role of leading professional. In this the headteacher is at the forefront of professional knowledge and developments and uses this expertise to provide a major professional influence on his or her colleagues.

New teachers need to recognise the approach of different headteachers to their job and the style in which they carry it out and to have appropriate expectations of headteachers and other senior staff.

(b) basis of decision-making

Irrespective of who participates in decision-making the basis of decision-making can be characterised as either rational or political. In rational decision-making it is the merit of the case which is preeminent. Rational decision-making is characteri[...] with overall aims of the organisation and the p[...] decision plays in that overall scheme, a need fo[...] mation and an impartial and objective approach [...] ments (Bush 1986). Political decision-making, on the other hand, recognises that the individuals involved in the decision either as decision-makers or largely affected by the decision are at least as important as the merits of the decision itself. Bargaining, negotiation and vested interests are features of political decision-making.

New teachers need to be aware of these two approaches to decision-making in the school which they join and to play their part accordingly if they are to influence decisions which concern them.

(c) organisational structure

This represents the control and co-ordination structure of the school. It includes how positions in the school relate to one another and the basic working rules of the organisation (Fidler 1992).

Organisations with a formal structure can, for simplicity, be divided into two major types—bureaucracies and collegial structures. In practice few organisations will be wholly consistent and of one type. They are likely to be a mixture, particularly at different levels.

A bureaucracy represents a formal ordering of positions in a hierarchy. Most organisations including most schools operate a structure which more closely resembles a bureaucracy rather than a collegial structure. Personnel within a school with a specialised function are grouped together under a section head who is accountable for the work of the section. These sections or departments are co-ordinated and controlled by more senior positions in the school. Although the reality may appear less authoritarian than the previous description, the formal accountabilities are likely to be those described. Whatever the formal organisation, the informal networks of communication, power, influence and control need also to be considered since they may be very different to the formal structure.

A collegial structure, on the other hand, relies on decision-making not by positional power but by peer groups working in a participative way. Mintzberg (1983) has proposed the term 'professional bureaucracy' to describe the situation where the positions of authority are arranged hierarchically but are occupied by members of the profession and there is participation in decision-making.

These features of schools as workplaces have implications for the preparation of teachers if they are to take their places as teachers in schools with the minimum of adaptation. Students will need to be rovided with some frameworks within which to analyse their experiences in schools. Any one school will illustrate a particular example of practice on each of these three and other aspects of organisational working but it may or may not be typical of other schools so students need to experience and analyse a range of schools if they are to be well-prepared to take their place in the school in which they are employed after training.

Two paradigms of teaching as a profession

Attempts to analyse professional activity, including teaching, have devised two alternative models (Schon 1983):

- technical rationality
- reflection-in-action.

Technical rationality assumes that professionals have theoretical knowledge which is applied to particular situations. The knowledge is acquired in a systematic way through empirical testing. The skills of the professional are needed to apply this knowledge to particular problems by diagnosing needs and selecting appropriate actions on the basis of theoretical knowledge. Although widely regarded as a theoretical description of the basis of professional practice there have been recent criticisms of this model. Glazer (1974) has drawn attention to the ambiguous and value-laden ends of the minor professions, such as teaching, which make the development of a scientific knowledge base problematic. Schein (1972) has developed a hierarchy of professional knowledge and skills:

- knowledge of the underlying theoretical base
- knowledge of the applied science of diagnosis and problem solving
- skills and attitudes concerning the actual performance of the service to the client.

This has implications for the order in which knowledge is acquired during training and leads to the separation of theory from practice. Schon's (1983) criticisms of technical rationality as the prevailing paradigm of professional practice led him to propose an alternative—reflection-in-action.

He referred to the knowledge which professionals have and which is demonstrated by the way in which they carry out their work—knowing-in-action. He postulated that in solving problems and dealing with new situations, professionals instantaneously think through alternative ways of tackling the problem and select an appropriate solution—reflection-in-action. Professionals may act in this way but be unable to verbalise their thought processes. Handal and Lauvas (1987) use the term 'practical theory' for knowing-in-action.

These contrasting accounts of professional practice have implications for the preparation of professionals.

For technical rationality the professional curriculum would start with a study of the underlying discipline before moving on to theoretical ideas on diagnosis and problem solving and finally to practice the skills of the profession on clients in the field. There are some unacknowledged discontinuities in moving from an idealised theoretical framework for diagnosing and solving problems to the practicalities of tackling singular, irregular, specific problems instantaneously.

Reflection-in-action acknowledges the need for basic knowledge but also recognises the need of professionals to create their own framework to conceptualise their own practice.

> Professional education should be redesigned to combine the teaching of applied science with coaching in the artistry of reflection-in-action (Schon 1987 p.xii).

The crucial difference between the two approaches concerns the extent to which there are problematic processes involved in conceptualising and framing appropriate teaching programmes for which those who organise training can provide more than opportunities for teaching and learning on a trial and error basis.

Some, following critical theory (Van Manen 1977), seek to extend reflection on practice beyond reflection on the means of achieving prescribed ends to an emancipatory critical reflection on the worth of the whole enterprise (Zeichner and Liston 1987). Here the term reflection will be used as in the framework developed by Schon (1983, 1987).

Implications for teacher preparation

What then are the components of teacher preparation and how and where should they be provided?

There are some prerequisites which are needed before expert practical teaching can be achieved:

- knowledge and understanding of subject matter
- knowledge and understanding of theory and techniques of pedagogy
- knowledge and understanding of how schools function.

There are also some knowledge areas in which there are general guidelines but individuals need to engage in their practice to more fully appreciate and internalise:

- design of teaching programmes
- selection of material and techniques for specific instances
- lesson delivery.

The pre-requisites are those elements of the craft, science, art, or profession which are theoretical schema or standard techniques. Teaching then consists of designing teaching programmes, selecting material and teaching techniques for a specific instance and delivering a lesson. This action can be planned on the basis of theoretical knowledge but this needs enhancement from the learning which can come from carrying out these operations in a variety of situations.

Whilst there is worthwhile theoretical knowledge which informs the process of teaching, teaching is not a science. The process is much more the operation of judgement based upon rather 'fuzzy' logic. This element has led to the concept of the reflective practitioner. The teacher capable of articulating and reflecting on his or her experience and creating personal mental schemata into which to fit this experience represents the height of professional practice.

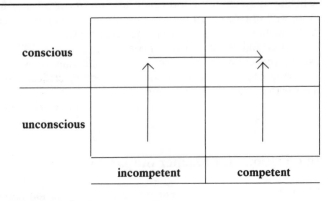

Figure 2.1 Johari window of competence and consciousness

Using a form of Johari window (Luft 1961) (Figure 2.1) to illustrate, the professional training process consists of moving trainees from the state of incompetence to the state of competence after the change from the unconscious to the conscious articulation of their thought processes.

The first element is a good knowledge and understanding of the subject matter which is to be taught.

The need for partnerships

It is clear that no single institution is in a position to provide all the components of the preparation process. Higher education institutions should be competent to provide the subject matter and theoretical parts of the process. They should also be able to provide the generalised practice in planning teaching programmes and lesson preparation. However, only schools can provide the opportunity to watch exemplary practitioners, to practice class teaching and to experience working in schools. Thus two institutions are needed but it is in the area of integrating theoretical concepts with experience and building up personal schemes within which to store experience where partnerships between HEIs and schools and between lecturers and teachers are needed.

Evolving partnerships

Three recent sources are drawn upon to examine the nature of evolving partnerships between schools, teachers and HEIs in this section. Firstly, a project in the 1980s studied four innovative courses which were more school-centred (Furlong et al. 1988). Secondly, a large-scale survey of teacher training courses was carried out in the early 1990s (Miles et al. 1993). Thirdly, a wide-ranging professional study of changes to teacher training in Northern Ireland attempted to analyse competences required of teachers and where and at what stage in their training and early career teachers should acquire these competences (DENI 1993a, 1993b).

Following CATE criteria in the 1980s some courses of teacher preparation adopted designs which were more school-based. Four such PGCE courses, two primary and two secondary, were studied by Furlong et al. (1988). They anticipated that in addition to spending more time in schools, the course design would more closely resemble a training in reflection-in-action. Following Schon (1983) they regarded a traditional training course as adopting a 'rationalist rule-governed model of professional activity' (p.123). They argued that a move to a reflective practitioner model of teaching would require the acquisition of new knowledge in new ways. The research group identified four levels of training:

(a) direct practice—'development of understanding, judgement

and skills through direct practical experience in the
classroom, school or community context' (p.130)

(b) indirect practice—'derived from talks, books, videos,
discussions'

(c) practical principles—'acquisition of knowledge of the
principles behind different professional practices and
reflection on their use and justification' (p.130). This is
acquired through reflection or direct teaching

(d) disciplinary theory—'to make explicit and critically
examine such value judgements and theoretical assumptions
by reference to the foundation disciplines' (p.131). It is
argued that this both provides knowledge and also may help
reflection and analysis.

They also examined the location of each element and the personnel
who might assist in its development. They noted that over and above
the amount of time spent in school, its arrangement could be significant. A pattern which involved the alternation between short periods
in school and short periods in an HEI each week were more likely to
be conducive to reflection on practice than longer periods in school
alone.

The customary division of responsibility would require that
school experience and teachers would contribute to (a) whilst HEIs
and curriculum and method tutors would contribute to (b), (c) and
(d). However, moving to a school-based approach, with longer
periods spent in school, requires teachers to make a greater contribution. For this to be successful it is clear that for all partners in the
operation there needs to be, at the level of principle, agreement on
the:

- model to be used for teaching
- model to be used for training
- extent of their relative contributions.

To bring this into operation there will need to be joint planning and
contributions from both partners.

Such changes to the approach to training will require new knowledge and skills from all the contributors to training. Thus development will be required for both HE tutors and teachers. Arguably the
greatest development is that required for teachers. They need to:

- develop skills of mentoring
- acquire or refresh their knowledge base
- develop their ability to articulate their reflective practice.

In commenting on the demands of this extended role Furlong et al. (1988) remark:

> That task demands both *skills in the sophisticated analysis of teaching and skills in the training of students which are widely considered to form quite distinct areas of professional expertise.* The move, step by step, to making teachers progressively more responsible for the training in classroom teaching of critically reflective professionals, thus makes progressively more demands on them which, by virtue of their own professional training and experience as classroom teachers, they cannot be expected to fulfil (p.190).

From the experience of the four courses they were studying, the research team warned:

> whatever the training institution may expect, teacher tutors are, in general, currently undertaking little more than supervision of a traditional kind (p.190).

They cautioned against a partnership which was too ambitious and under-resourced. It is possible to design a course pattern which may meet the needs of students in training very well but poses too great a demand on teachers and tutors. A complex arrangement which apportions responsibilities between teachers and tutors will need to try to ensure that all are clear about their respective roles. As Furlong et al. comment:

> Somewhere, a balance has to be struck between an ideal of joint training and a practically effective structure (p.191).

Where a process requires expertise from a number of sources, these can either be provided by a complex pattern of contributions from a number of individuals or by developing the knowledge of a smaller number of contributors. The latter requires a substantial investment in development and there are pressures, therefore, to programme a complex arrangement of contributions from specialists. In contributing to courses for preparing reflective practitioners each of these specialists has to play a part in assisting the teacher to reflect on his or her practice from each specialist perspective.

Later evidence of a more representative kind is provided by the Modes of Teacher Education (MOTE) research project. This included a survey of teacher training courses conducted in 1990–91 (Miles et al. 1993). This covered 85 per cent of courses including BEds, PGCEs and Articled Teacher Schemes. It discovered that the reflective practitioner model of teaching was the most common, a small minority used a competency model and a traditional model was used by a sizeable minority. Partnerships between schools and HEIs were in evidence. However, these covered a wide spectrum from a 'high partnership' involving teachers in subject application, assessment of students and joint planning, to a 'low partnership' which was of a much more token kind.

Whilst for courses as a whole, the location of some elements could be polarised—subject studies in HEIs and teaching practice in schools—all other elements had some courses which involved both schools and HEIs. Teachers supervised and assessed teaching practice in most courses and helped plan school experience in about half of the courses. Only about a quarter of courses were paying schools for supervision and this tended to be associated with teachers taking a more major role in interviewing, teaching, supervision and assessment.

When the amount of time which students spent in schools was compared with the involvement of teachers in training, the project found:

> While there is some evidence ... that large amounts of school-based training may mean teachers are more fully involved in the planning, teaching and assessment of *school experience*, the survey data suggest that increasing the amount of time in schools does not, necessarily, enhance the role of teachers in *all aspects* of the training process (p.297).

Miles et al. point out that this finding is consistent with HMI's findings (HMI 1991) that increasing the time in schools does not necessarily enhance the quality of school experience and the nature of the relationships between HEIs and schools.

A major review of teacher training in Northern Ireland (DENI 1993a, 1993b) has looked at the acquisition of teaching competences on a longer timescale. The review considered whether they should be acquired in training, and if so, whether in schools or HEIs, and also whether they should be acquired in induction in a first teaching post or in subsequent professional development. The working parties which considered the issues were jointly made up to represent schools and teacher training institutions with some interested outsiders.

Figure 2.2 attempts to summarise a more detailed breakdown of the competence elements in the report (DENI 1993a). The report makes the caveat that 'in the short time available to us, our conclusions have in many cases been somewhat arbitrary, and we wish them to be read as both tentative and preliminary' (p.13).

It should be noted that many competences require contributions from both HEIs and schools and may extend beyond initial training. This, combined with changing major and minor roles, requires close

Competence	Location	Phase
Professional knowledge		
knowledge and understanding of children and their learning	HE/s	ITT/i
subject knowledge	HE	ITT
knowledge of the curriculum	HE/s	ITT/i/fpd
knowledge of the educational system	HE/s	ITT/i
knowledge of the teacher's role	HE/s	itt/I/FPD
Professional skills		
subject application	he/S	ITT/i/FPD
classroom methodology	he/S	itt/I/fpd
class management	he/S	itt/I
assessment and recording	he/S	itt/I/fpd
the wider role	he/S	I/FPD

Key

Location
HE   Higher education institutions
S   Schools
Phase
ITT   Initial training
I   Induction
FPD Further professional development

Major/minor roles
Capital letters indicate a major role
Small letters indicate a minor role

Figure 2.2 Professional competences which characterise the successful teacher

partnership and collaboration between schools and teacher training institutions. The report points out that:

> The fact that the development of most of the competences clearly requires experience and practice in the classroom does not necessarily mean that the school in which the practice takes place should have the prime responsibility for promoting or assessing these competences. Indeed the tutoring, guidance and support to which we refer is of the kind currently provided during ITT by the HEIs (p.14).

Managing partnerships

As the previous discussion has shown only a craft model of teaching would not require some kind of partnership between HEIs and schools and tutors and teachers. However, despite the requirements of Circulars 9/92 and 14/93 there are many choices to be made concerning the form of partnership which is set up.

This discussion assumes that the leading partner in the first instance will be the HEI since that is the institution which has teacher training as its first priority. Any move to renegotiate pre-existing arrangements with schools has to take account of local circumstances and be part of the institutional strategies of both partners (Fidler 1989b; Fidler et al. 1991). There is a great danger that external pressures will push institutions into reactive decisions that do not have any long term chance of success. As revisions to the National Curriculum have demonstrated, the problem of unworkable legislation has to be faced sooner or later. Whatever the legislation, it should be remembered that improving the training of teachers is the ultimate aims of HEIs, tutors and students, schools, teachers and pupils and meets the longer term needs of the educational system. These are more important than blindly following legislation.

Nevertheless, properly conceived schemes of more-school-based training, adequately resourced and implemented with good will have much potential to increase the already high standards of teacher preparation. Any planning has to take account of existing arrangements with schools and the potential of both the HEI and schools to change. All change takes time but major change needs both lengthy and thorough preparation and much time to implement. Plans should be examined for their long-term sustainability and all planning should face the possibility that some changes are simply not possible at a particular point in time.

What then are the considerations involved in planning for a greater degree of school-based training? There are considerations of:

- co-operation and communication,
- potential of schools and teachers
- potential of HEIs and tutors
- resourcing.

Co-operation and communication

There is expected to be joint planning of training by representatives from schools and HEIs. Any such planning should start from an agreement about the model of teaching which is being used as the outcome of training. The degree to which it is conceived as a craft, a science, an art or a profession and whether or not the model of profession involves reflecting on practice will need extensive discussion with examples. Following from this there should also be agreement about the model of training and who is providing which elements of that training. Any such agreement is likely to be with some representatives of schools and teachers. Such are likely to be senior staff particularly in primary schools, so any putative agreement needs to be checked with those who are likely to be concerned in classrooms and lecture rooms for its acceptability.

Following agreement at the principles stage, details have to be planned and all involved have to be fully informed and prepared for the parts they have to play. HMI (1991) draw attention to examples where teachers in classrooms were unaware of, or had failed to fully appreciate, their role. Although communication can never hope to be 100 per cent successful, a variety of approaches—familiarisation conferences, written guidelines and visits from tutors—should all be used in an attempt to raise awareness, understanding and commitment to the highest possible level.

Furlong et al. (1988) and HMI (1991) regard serial experience in school, alternate short periods in school and in college, as a particularly valuable form of school experience. This is usually organised by a tutor and involves students carrying out investigative or other assigned tasks in school in co-operation with a teacher and discussion of them back in college.

> Its major purpose, in both primary and secondary courses, is to enable close and precise links to be made between institution-based work and classroom practice (para 35 pp.18–19)

Any discussion of possibilities should involve a thorough examination of the benefits and drawbacks for each of the partners and a consideration of the level of resources which will be available to fund the process. In addition to the level of resources being appropriate there is a need to ensure that the logistical arrangements are not too complicated. As Furlong et al. (1988) pointed out

> For many complex, practical reasons, communication between the two parties can be difficult and the course pattern may really be too complex in its demands on collaboration for what is feasible in the circumstances. A lack of clarity in the precise definition of roles is also a recurring element in the picture we have formed. Somewhere, a balance has to be struck between an ideal of joint training and a practically effective structure (p.191).

Summing up the importance of co-operative planning of courses HMI (1991) wrote:

> A consistent finding over some years from inspection is that the overall quality of training is not a direct product of the amount of time spent in schools or of a particular pattern of school experience but rather of the quality of the teachers and the

relationships between schools and training institutions (para 37 pp.19–20).

Potential of schools and teachers

It is clear from HMI experience (HMI 1991; OFSTED 1993) that school experience which takes place in poor schools or with poor teachers is unlikely to produce valuable experiences for student teachers. Whilst this may seem obvious, it has to be recognised that headteachers, particularly in primary schools, may choose teachers to host student teachers for other reasons than their suitability as models of good teaching. Schools have as their first priority the education of children and there may be a need not unduly to disrupt the education of particular groups of children.

> The quality of school experience often depended largely on the quality of the individual teacher to whom the student was assigned. Such teachers were usually selected by the headteacher, not the college. These teachers will assume particular importance when the school-based element of initial training is increased (OFSTED 1993 p.32).

Where students do not spend the majority of their time with one teacher, as is typically the case in secondary schools, the problem of one teacher as role model is much reduced. This is important as HMI (OFSTED 1993) have drawn attention to a widespread criticism from new teachers that their training did not include sufficient opportunities to watch and discuss good examples of teaching.

This requirement would be true for any school experience but for any move towards expecting teachers to be mentors and help students to reflect on their practice there are two added requirements. Such teachers should be able to reflect on their own practice and also have the personal skills to be able to assist students in acquiring the skills to reflect on their own practice.

> Successful teachers of children are not necessarily successful teachers of adults (HMI 1991 p.25)

Finally, the teachers who meet all these requirements have to be willing to take on this commitment. Whilst some teachers who are willing and do not have all these skills yet, may develop these skills with appropriate assistance, it should not be assumed that all such teachers are capable of acquiring such skills.

The schools and teachers who meet these criteria will need to receive appropriate forms of training and development initially for their new role and support as their experience evolves. The final requirement is that such teachers will need an appropriate amount of free time in order to be able to work with students. In partnerships where teachers are not expected to act as mentors, they will still be expected to play a major part in assessing students and training and support will also be needed for this function.

Potential of HEIs and tutors

The HEI's contribution should be complementary to that of the school. For undergraduate courses they provide subject knowledge. Recent research on teaching (Bennett and Carre 1993) has emphasised the importance of a sound understanding of subject matter in order to teach well. Although as HMI (OFSTED 1993) point out:

> Good depth of knowledge was not by itself enough to ensure successful lessons (p.19).

For most courses HEI tutors provide education studies knowledge and curriculum application. The teaching of the disciplines of educational studies has proved problematic. According to McIntyre (1993) students find educational studies of most value if tutors clearly signal the implications of the disciplines for teachers. He finds that tutors are reluctant to do this for fear of oversimplifying. However, he makes the telling point that if experts are diffident about pointing out such implications for fear of over-simplifying is it any wonder that students are at least as reticent in trying to apply their knowledge from the disciplines. McIntyre defends the continuing importance of the disciplines for reflective practitioners:

> acceptance of theory as process need not, and should not in my view, limit the importance which we attach to theory as content (p.41).

> In order to theorise fruitfully, student teachers need appropriate content about which they can theorise (p.47).

As HMI (1991) wrote:

> The quality of the involvement of higher education tutors is a major factor. At best they bring a level of subject and curricular expertise and a comparative view of training, based on contact with other students and schools, which complement the contribution of the school (pp.28–9).

To carry out their new role and to support teachers in school, HEI tutors will need to be chosen for their personal qualities, their knowledge of educational and curriculum studies and less for their teaching experience as supervision of this is progressively taken on by schools. Tutors will need appropriate forms of development in order to take on this new role.

Resourcing partnerships

The Northern Ireland review of ITT (DENI 1993a) recognised that:

> School-based initial training is likely to have maintenance costs above those of conventional training and at least in the early stages there will be development costs (p.26).

Thus it is unrealistic to imagine that schools can be adequately funded for training by merely transferring money from HEIs. Extra money will also be required to improve training.

Whatever the precise expectations of teachers they need time for:

- professional development
- work with students
- collaboration with HE lecturers in course planning.

Some estimate of this time can be gained from the observation of Furlong et al. (1988):

> we can report that only in the course where funding was most generous (i.e. in Leeds with 0.2 teachers per student) was the degree of resourcing considered adequate by teachers, heads and college personnel (p.191).

As Fitch (1994) points out, CATE and the Government have been willing to prescribe course content and length of time in schools but have been quite vague about the resourcing of schools for the extra commitment they are expected to undertake. The only hint from DFE (1993a) is that there should be marginal extra funding for the marginal extra work. He surmises that 'free market economics' will be used to see what the market will bear in terms of what schools will accept and HEIs can afford to pay.

As a contribution to the debate, and one suspects as a way of trying to raise the stakes in view of 'the reluctance of HEIs to face up to economic reality' (p.370), Shaw (1992b) has produced a calculation for the cost of ten students in a secondary school. This covers training, classroom observation, meetings with trainees, materials, etc. which totals some £1,250 per student but this includes one-off costs for staff training of £150 per student. The largest single element is supply cover to release staff to observe and debrief students. She clearly views the present contribution to schools from the £3,750 which HEIs receive for each student as quite inadequate.

Fitch (1994) suggests two methods of distributing resources to partnership schools:

1. Directly costing and paying for the time taken by schools in mentoring.
2. Dividing the student income in proportion to the relative amount of time spent in schools and HE.

But he cautions against using time as the main element in modelling the training process. There may be economies of scale which undermine a simple pro-rata distribution of resources.

A more complex variant of the second method has been proposed by Wright (1993). He suggests taking each of eight cost headings:

- teaching costs
- student travel
- library and equipment
- consumables
- coursewares
- administration costs
- staff travel
- overhead/infrastructure costs

for the education of PGCE students and dividing each of these according to the relative costs incurred by schools and HEIs. A formula could then be used to distribute the sum which supports the education of each student according to the aggregate of these proportions. Unfortunately this would require much work and estimation in arriving at the current cost of each of these budget heads so that the sums could be divided and added.

Such calculations would be likely to be viewed with some suspicion by both parties since they are very subjective and as the calculations of Shaw (1992b) demonstrate, costs are likely to be inflated as a bargaining counter. Since the base income for educating students which is provided to HEIs is an arbitrary sum rather than being needs based, any proposal to recompense schools on the basis of actual costs appears to be inconsistent with the rationale of this base funding and so some division of this sum in a market situation appears to be the most likely outcome.

As HMI (1991) cautioned, in transferring funds from HE to schools:

> Some care would be needed to ensure that the higher education base was not reduced to a point where it could not make its essential contribution (p.35).

Part 2
Working in
partnership

3   The PGCE and the training of primary teachers

Joan Whitehead and Tor Foster with Mary Blight

Introduction

Preparing graduate students to become primary teachers has always been a challenge but it is one which has increased significantly with the introduction of the National Curriculum and its associated testing arrangements. Still other challenges have been posed by the uncertainties surrounding the government's deliberations over the future form and content of primary training, as well as by debates within the educational world itself about the organisation and philosophy of primary education (DES 1992b). The central thrust of Government policy has been towards the increased involvement of practising teachers in the training of new recruits to the profession, a policy direction originally signalled in Circular 3/84, developed in Circular 24/89 and assuming a new and more radical form in Circular 14/93. Whilst both of the earlier circulars had encouraged partnerships between higher education institutions and schools in the training of student teachers, the new circular and the Education Bill, before Parliament at the time of writing, for the first time make it possible for the governing bodies of primary schools to provide courses of initial training either themselves or in partnership with higher education. Only through the continued involvement of an HEI will it however be possible for students to continue to gain a postgraduate certificate.

The other policy direction accompanying the move towards an enhanced role for schools in training teachers is the redefinition of the nature of teaching as work, with the implicit assumption that teaching itself can be defined through a set of practical teaching competences. Although the identification of competences appropriate to the beginning teacher is important, what is omitted is any reference to an overall model of sound and effective professional practice. Our own view is that 'the sum total of competences may add up to something less than an effective, imaginative and stimulating primary practitioner' (UWE 1993) a teacher moreover who understands and can articulate the basis of such practice. In our own course provision we are therefore attempting both to further our partnerships with schools as well as to develop professional competences in our students which link with our ongoing commitment to principles of reflective pedagogy.

Within this changing context, the account which follows describes the Primary PGCE at the University of the West of England and our own philosophy of teacher education. We then discuss various partnership developments and in particular draw on an account by one of our school partners, a nursery headteacher seconded part-time to work with us as a teacher fellow. We conclude by identifying a number of issues raised by such developments which we see as necessary to take into account when moving to implement the new statutory requirements.

The context of the primary PGCE course

The course we currently offer prepares students to teach in either the early years (3–7) or the later years (7–11), with the former route offered on both a full-time and part-time basis. It is one of a number of award routes within the Faculty's Modular Programme for Initial Teacher Training. Along with the other award routes it has been designed to accord with the Faculty's commitment to reflective pedagogic principles whilst also having regard to the regulatory framework of Circular 24/89, the requirements of the National Curriculum, and the move towards competences signalled in Circular 9/92 and subsequently adopted for primary training in Circular 14/93.

These principles which inform and underpin the PGCE imply an approach to professional competence beyond the subject knowledge and skills necessary to teach the primary curriculum. They include the fostering of broader professional qualities and capacities such that students during their one year of initial training learn to make informed judgements, to appreciate that 'knowing how' needs to be underpinned by 'knowing why' and that the critical reflection in which they are required to engage is integral to their academic, personal and professional development as primary teachers. This process of informed reflection, whilst begun during this initial but highly pressurised period of training is seen as laying the foundations for, and as the first stage in, career-long professional development.

Given the constraints imposed by the 36-week course (which will only be marginally relieved by the extra two weeks added by Circular 14/93) the Faculty regards it as imperative for students to recognise their need for further professional development during and after their induction year. In addition, therefore, to the acquisition of core pedagogic competences, the PGCE course aims to generate in students a commitment to life-long learning, and a willingness to reflect upon and act throughout their careers to improve their professional practice to the benefit of those they teach.

In order to realise these commitments the Faculty has worked with teachers in a range of partnership developments. Whilst many of these have been operating for a number of years the Secretary of State's speech to the North of England Conference in January 1992 provided further impetus. It was this which added momentum to the Faculty's formulation of the following precepts of partnership:

> an integrated approach to training which reflects an appropriate balance of school and HE experience, and ensures reciprocity in the exchange of expertise,

> the fostering of a partnership ethos in all elements of design and delivery, including joint planning arrangements, and the sharing of responsibility for developing students' competences,

> a commitment from both partners to an extended partnership, continuing beyond initial training to induction support and appropriate professional development.

These precepts have guided the Faculty's partnership developments which are constantly evolving in response both to our own monitoring and evaluation of existing provision as well as to the externally imposed political agenda. Our desire annually to review and improve provision necessarily has to be set within available resources which have influenced both the nature and extent of the developments in which we have engaged.

The Faculty's commitment to partnership and school-focused training is, however, long standing and is evidenced by our original Primary PGCE award exceeding the minimum number of days in school required by Circular 24/89, whilst our current award already meets the 90 days in school required by Circular 14/93. In supporting a maximal definition of partnership we do not regard the site of learning, be it Faculty or school, as itself the guarantee of effective professional preparation. Rather, as HMI report on school-based training (HMI 1991) indicates, of crucial importance is the need for coherence and for those involved in the training, to be aware of, and prepared for, their respective roles and responsibilities across the training sites. We have made some progress in so preparing our school partners by the provision of a limited amount of supply cover to release teachers for preparatory work with students in advance of one of the periods of school experience. This is an area in which we recognise the need to develop our practice still further and look forward to support from transitional funding to make possible the fuller preparation of the teachers with whom we work. To date we have not gone down the road of creating teacher tutors nor have we involved ourselves in any cash transfers to schools for the payment of supervision.

In many ways therefore our Primary PGCE operates within a relatively conventional definition of partnership as a relationship between equals [schools and HEIs] (CNAA) and involving 'mutual respect' (CATE) through the participation of schools in planning and management, in the selection of students for entry, and in contributing to (whilst not yet assuming a leading role in), the students' training and assessment. The course has nevertheless been acknowledged as offering students a high quality training with the various dimensions of partnership being incremental in their effect. We are by no means complacent about the course since we readily acknowledge from both our own student evaluations and evidence nationally that such a truncated period of training has endemic weaknesses and poses a number of significant challenges.

Principles underpinning the course

We are then working in a context in which expectations of what the beginning teacher should know, and be able to do, have increased significantly. HMI (OFSTED 1993) have suggested that primary initial teacher training (ITT) courses have not always succeeded in covering all aspects sufficiently, particularly in terms of curriculum knowledge. There is evidence that Newly Qualified Teachers (NQTs) feel less confident about their preparation in 'foundation' subjects than in 'core' subjects and that students feel particularly limited in their knowledge of technology. There is also significant dissatisfaction expressed by students in their preparation to use information technology in the classroom.

We are also aware of the debate over whether primary teachers should be generalists or specialists. It is apparent that although NQTs will be selected for first appointments mainly on their abilities as generalist teachers (OFSTED 1993), they will very quickly be given curriculum leadership and it will be expected that their ITT course will have given students some preparation for this new role.

In an attempt to meet these concerns and changing demands, we have each year made adjustments to our course—improving the content and developing new styles of teaching and learning. Later in the text examples of such modifications are given when the development of a closer and more complex relationship with school colleagues is discussed.

However, at the outset, it is important to make clear that the Primary PGCE course at UWE is based on a number of interrelated principles which include:

- a belief in the importance of the student as an autonomous learner and reflective practitioner
- a commitment to student entitlement and on-going evaluation of all aspects of the course
- a commitment to integrated learning, and
- a commitment to partnership with schools.

As indicated by the first principle, it is our aim that students should develop into autonomous thinking practitioners who are grounded in values and knowledge that will sustain them and be developed through their teaching careers. Thus our aim is to empower students; to develop in them an ability to reflect and a confidence to take action as a result of their considered judgements.

Where NQTs have experienced a lack of job satisfaction or been identified as ineffective, HMI have noted that many displayed 'little capacity for self-appraisal and, consequently, for self improvement' and 'an inability to respond to support and advice' as well as having 'entrenched attitudes and communication difficulties' (OFSTED 1993). It is hoped that our course in design and practice—with its focus on reflection, collaboration and communication—helps students to avoid such pitfalls.

The second principle—commitment to student entitlement—is equally important. We are conscious that many of our students have invested a huge amount both financially and emotionally in the PGCE course. Some have left well-established jobs to make a career change. Many are mature students who have previously held positions of considerable responsibility. These are factors which we cannot afford to, and would not want to, ignore.

Our students are entitled to a high quality course. Thus, just as we encourage our students to reflect and make judgements about all aspects of their pedagogy, so too it follows that such evaluation should apply to all aspects of the course. Written evaluations, both formative and summative, are made by the students throughout the course and are passed on to relevant tutors for comment and appropriate action. Additionally, there are both formal ways (meetings with representatives of each tutor group) and more informal ways (discussion with individual students) in which we keep abreast of how the course is going and the nature of students' perceived needs. If tutors as well as our school colleagues involved in course delivery are, and are to be perceived to be, reflective practitioners, then it is important for us to be both accountable and flexible in delivering the course.

The third principle—commitment to integrated learning—is related to the first two. We have adopted a 'social constructivist' model of learning, which can be traced back to Vygotsky (1962), believing that it is only through making connections between all aspects of the course and discussion of them that students can become reflective and knowledgeable practitioners. So while the course can be identified as having three distinct parts (curriculum studies, education studies and school experience) the inter-relatedness between the three is continually emphasised. School tasks, assignments and seminar discussions are all designed to bring together knowledge and experience gained in different parts of the course and at the various sites of learning (the university, schools and elsewhere).

In Vygotsky's terminology we are attempting to move students on through their 'zones of proximal development' both by appropriate tutor or teacher intervention and by encouraging collaborative learning, whereby students learn from and with each other. The 'zone of proximal development' has been defined by Wood (1988) as the gap 'between unassisted and assisted competence'. It is clear that such assistance or 'scaffolding' of the learning experience can be provided by school staff, university staff and fellow students and our approach is intended to allow for and encourage such learning to take place. It is through such an integrated approach that we make most effective use of the limited time available and the students receive the quality training to which they are entitled.

Partnership in the primary PGCE

The fourth principle—a commitment to partnership with school colleagues—is increasingly crucial as the basis for achieving the preceding three. Partnership with schools is both the most obvious and the most problematic aspect of a good ITT course. It is obvious because students become confident practitioners by being in schools where they can both observe good practice and develop their skills as teachers. As HMI (OFSTED 1993) have recognised, school experience can be a lottery for students and yet the delivery of a quality course depends vitally on providing a supportive, appropriate and challenging school experience. It is only when colleagues in schools and teacher training institutions are working in a complementary way that successful training can be guaranteed. But it is also problematic, for a number of reasons. These include the 'traditional' divide between teacher training institutions and schools with all that that suggests about poor communication and lack of mutual trust and understanding (Barber 1993). There are also practical and logistical difficulties concerned with allocating a large cohort of students (in our case 120) to several school placement sites during a 36-week course. Additionally, when working with a large number of schools, it is difficult to be certain that the support offered is always appropriate.

However, the increasing demands on ITT courses mentioned previously have necessitated greater involvement with schools in a far wider range of activities. If each of these different school-based activities is to meet the third principle and be integrated with all other aspects of the course, a successful partnership between university tutors and school colleagues is vital.

Such a partnership must be based on a shared understanding of the nature of the course. Unfortunately, the traditional dichotomy between theory and practice is one which lives on in the world outside the university. It is expounded in the media by those who favour an apprenticeship, school-based teacher training model. Despite HMI recognition (OFSTED 1993) that teacher training institutions have, over the past few years, linked the content of education studies more closely to work in schools, critics perpetuate the myth that institutions offer a diet of 'ologies', theories which are unrelated to practical teaching. Teachers in our partner schools may share these misconceptions especially if their own training took place some time ago. The challenge for the university is to inform school colleagues about, and involve them in, the design, content and aims of the course.

The quality of our communication with schools is, therefore, vital. We have recently reviewed our written course material. It has been our practice to provide the same guidelines for school experience to students, teachers and university tutors thus enabling all concerned to gain an overall perspective on goals and expectations. During the past year attempts have been made to make these documents more user-friendly through careful editing after consultation with all the parties involved. Communication has also been improved by providing schools with a summary of information, in the form of a regularly updated profile, about each of the students who will be visiting the school. Schools have welcomed this initiative and we see it as the beginning stage of a student profiling system which is being developed at the university. HMI (HMI 1988) have recommended that profiling would be useful in giving schools details about students' strengths and weaknesses and would build bridges between training and employment. We have adopted this idea but have started it one stage earlier and initial feedback indicates that this sharing of knowledge has been appreciated by all parties.

Increasingly we have encouraged students to consult with class teachers about the appropriateness of their ideas for their written assignments and various school-based tasks. Teachers can give practical advice which is greatly valued by the students. The benefits of such teacher involvement are great especially where the class-teacher is confident and supportive. But, as HMI (OFSTED 1993) noted, this greater involvement of teachers can lead to inequity in terms of student experience. To minimize this we have attempted to be explicit about the nature of student tasks and assignments and how we would like teachers to become involved.

There is a tension here between trying to provide sufficient and clear information and not overwhelming teachers with too much paperwork. Ideally, we would want to place a description of these school-related tasks in the context of the whole course, including the principles on which the course is based, but, we have to be realistic about the amount of time we can expect teachers to give to studying course material.

However good our written communication is, it is the face to face communication that sustains and develops positive and fruitful working relationships. We make a considerable effort to arrange meetings between school and university staff to plan and evaluate different aspects of the course. Thus, for example, before each school experience, we invite school colleagues to the university to meet us and the students to exchange information, to illuminate aspects of the course for teachers and to provide a reassuring ice-breaker for the students.

Good communication regarding school experience has been particularly important where the nature of the planned experience differs from that likely to have been undertaken by the class teachers during their own training. This is best exemplified by our recently established group school experience. This one week experience, which was introduced three years ago, has a different focus from the other two school experiences. Students are required to work in teams in a classroom and the emphasis is on joint planning and evaluation. In addition, each student acts as a curriculum leader in his or her specialist subject. The success of this intensive experience depends crucially on significant support from school colleagues who both fully understand the aims and are committed to them and particularly to the notion of collaborative teaching.

Selecting appropriate school colleagues to work with us on this venture was a lengthy and time consuming process. Telephone calls were made to potentially supportive teachers, followed by detailed exploratory letters. For those teachers who eventually agreed to participate, funds were made available to provide supply cover so that they could spend half a day at the university, meeting the students and spending time with them for joint planning of the experience. The success of this element of our course, and of our ability to communicate our intentions about it, can be judged by the willingness of so many of our school colleagues to repeat the experience. We have continued to seek ways of improving the communication. For example, each participating school now receives a report in which one of the previous year's students provides a reflection on the experience. Of equal importance is the way in which school colleagues have felt able to participate in the development of modifications. For example, as a result of consultations and mindful of the needs of students, we have now added an additional focus, the use of information technology, to the experience.

This direct involvement of school colleagues in the design and development of our course highlights another important element in a successful partnership—shared ownership. If there is to be an effective working partnership, then all concerned—both students and university and school staff—must feel that account is taken, in the course design, of their views, knowledge and experience. Evidence of our willingness to share ownership is provided by the way in which modifications have recently been made to one school experience as a result of a consensus of teacher opinion. After a two-year trial we expanded the period of the group school experience from one week to two and we reduced the number of students working in a team to a maximum of four as suggested by school colleagues.

But the question of ownership is a difficult one. For schools to be true partners they need to be more involved in course development at all stages. To an extent we hope to encourage this through management structures. Headteachers from 'partner' schools are members of the course management committee which meets regularly to review the course and advise on developments. This committee is seen as an open forum for a genuine exchange of information and ideas. Opinions and ideas expressed at these meetings have been an important influence on ongoing course development.

However the limitations of this involvement are clear as only a tiny proportion of heads can be involved in the course management committee and the majority of partner schools are excluded. This is especially the case for primary ITT courses where there are significantly more schools involved than with secondary ITT courses.

One of the approaches we have adopted to give more schools greater ownership of the course is to involve school colleagues in the student admissions interviewing procedure. HMI (OFSTED 1993) make reference to the shared responsibility that should be taken by schools and universities for selecting appropriate candidates who are likely to become successful teachers. While shared responsibility could be achieved by joint interviews at the university, many of ours take place in partner schools. Prospective students spend most of a day in a classroom before being interviewed by the headteacher and a university tutor. This approach has proved popular with prospective students and with class teachers who have had an opportunity to contribute to the decision making by providing comments on the students prior to interview and have gained a greater sense of owner-ship of the course.

Despite the pressure of externally imposed changes and the resulting time constraints on both us and on school colleagues, new initiatives are underway to provide further improvements to extend the partnership.

One such initiative concerns the developing role of classteachers as 'mentors' to students. At present we are still operating the 'old' model of school experience tutoring whereby the student is sup-ported in the classroom by the classteacher and is visited regularly by a university tutor. However within this model, we are developing ways of enhancing the classteacher's input. We consistently encour-age open discussion between all three parties (the student, the teacher and the tutor) and we attempt to ensure that all visits by the tutor include such triangular discussion. This has done much to develop the classteacher's understanding of the pedagogical issues that can be discussed and to break down the 'them and us' feeling between schools and the university. We have also encouraged teachers to complete written evaluations on student performance, using the same 'feedback' forms as the tutor. This not only encour-ages teachers to give more systematic and structured feedback to students but also, since the tutor's completed forms serve as a model, it can be seen as informal mentor training for teachers who may be inexperienced in classroom observation. The need for such forms of mentor training is signalled in research (Edwards 1993) which indicates that school staff without training most often advise students on matters of discipline, curriculum content and classroom management and that they are far less likely to address aspects of children's learning.

Practice in partnership: teacher fellows

Whilst our partnership strategy on the Primary PGCE has been fundamentally evolutionary rather than revolutionary, a year ago the

Faculty embarked upon a more radical mode of partnership, albeit on a pilot basis across our initial training awards. This involved appointing a number of teacher fellows seconded from school either full or part time. Two were appointed to work on the Primary PGCE. The initiative, now extended to a second year, was motivated by our desire to examine the feasibility of joint HEI and school appointments in terms of the expertise each would bring to the training process. It was made possible by a number of posts in the Faculty becoming vacant as temporary contracts expired. A decision was then taken to look to secondments as a more appropriate staffing policy given the resource uncertainties created by government policy and the need therefore to give ourselves flexibility for the future.

Unlike the way in which mentors and teacher tutors are frequently appointed within schools which tends to be with minimal or no involvement by HEIs, the procedures followed for the appointment of the teacher fellows were the same as for the full-time academic staff in the Faculty. This we see as having a bearing on what has been a very successful dimension to our partnership developments although as with any policy it has not been without its problems.

In the account which follows we draw on a paper written by and discussion with Mary Blight who is one of our teacher fellows. Mary is a nursery school headteacher, seconded to work in partnership with us for two days a week. The pilot project was regarded by the Faculty as an exciting development and was welcomed as 'a creative and imaginative venture' by Mary herself. She had entered her sixth year as head of her school, the philosophy was established and the staff were committed and involved.

> I felt confident that the school situation was secure and stable and that it had a lot to offer as a 'training' establishment for future teachers. I also felt that it was an appropriate time for me to widen my professional horizon. I anticipated that staff in school would benefit from my professional development.

> Links with the university had been established over a number of years through participation in activities to support my own and other teachers' professional development and the school had been used for research by staff from UWE. Furthermore we had always been involved in the training of PGCE students through the provision of placements. I had led student discussions on aspects of early childhood education, had been involved in interviewing prospective PGCE students and was a member of the PGCE Course Management Committee. I was therefore very much aware both of the content of the course and of its intensity. The secondment seemed a natural and obvious

way of developing the work I was already doing and to which the school was committed.

The staff, the governing body, parents at the school and my Adviser in the LEA supported the secondment which the university negotiated with the LEA. Behind the euphoria of this innovative project, there was the inevitable apprehension of whether it would work 'in practice'. Doubts were cast by some headteacher colleagues questioning the feasibility of my dual roles but to me the secondment was a challenge and a privilege. It was a wonderful opportunity to widen my theoretical perspectives and to share my own expertise.

In securing her secondment we both recognised the importance of the support received from the LEA, governing body and school as well as the prior knowledge and respect each of us had for the expertise of the other. These factors were significant in helping guarantee a positive and constructive input to the training partnership as were the potential benefits each of us believed would accrue from the extended working relationship.

However, given that the PGCE course is so pressurised all staff need to be thoroughly conversant with its demands and to be able to respond appropriately and from the outset to students' diverse training needs. Hence all teacher fellows were given a week's induction in order to prepare them for their new responsibilities. One facet of this was the allocation of a mentor who was significant not just during the initial period of adjustment but also subsequently.

I would like to emphasise the importance of a mentor and of there being a match between the mentor and the person joining the Faculty regarding past experience and role within the education system. It was propitious that my mentor had been a headteacher himself. As such he was able to empathise with my feelings, expectations and frustrations throughout the secondment and to offer invaluable support. This support often came in a practical form but more crucially in discussing how we could transfer the particular skills we had developed as headteachers to our roles as tutors in higher education. I am aware of how easy it would have been to have felt de-skilled in the role of the tutor after being a headteacher. I have not, however, felt de-skilled, although I have at times felt frustrated by issues such as line management and curriculum planning.

My initial impression was that the majority of lecturers were concentrating on their own area of work, were intensely committed, and were working independently and in isolation. Was this part of the culture of higher education? It was very different from the school culture I was immersed in for the other part of my week. I was somewhat confused by the structure of the institution. I was confused by the matrix system of management and I often felt unsure as to whom I should consult over issues in order to gain a response. This became less hazy over the year but it was in these situations that I relied on the advice of my mentor in coming to terms with a Faculty considerably larger and more complex than my school.

Despite a certain familiarity with both the Faculty and the course, the cultural differences between the two contexts were apparent although less so with greater association and inclusion in more collaborative working relationships. What was necessary, however, was for university staff to continue to devote time and energy to induct teacher fellows into their roles and to learn the ways in which they could best draw on the expertise the teacher fellows had and vice versa.

Much of the knowledge, understanding and skills Mary possessed was, in fact, transferable from her work in schools and prior involvement with the course, although the foci of her activities were different.

As stated earlier, I was already aware of the PGCE course structure before I joined the Faculty as a teacher fellow. I felt the value of this as soon as I started my sessions as a group tutor. However it was a very different experience from having been a PGCE student, of having had a daughter on the course, and of having PGCE students in my school. It was a challenge which demanded the use of the intellectual, interpersonal and managerial skills I was used to employing in my school role. On reflection, when I initially thought of applying for the post of teacher fellow, I felt my skills as a classroom teacher would be my greatest asset. Within a short time I realised that it was the skills and strategies that I had used to build an effective team of motivated teachers that I was also to draw on in my role as group tutor.

The role was to bring me enormous job satisfaction. The demands were different from those made on me in school but the skills required were similar. Part of the role of group tutor required me to act as a model to future teachers, to utilise my interpersonal skills to run workshop sessions which were well planned, with clear intentions, professionally presented, and informed by appropriate theoretical and practical knowledge and skills. There was for me a further dimension to my role of group tutor which was to have students from my tutor group

placed in my school, a situation dissimilar from UWE group
tutors who were not so exposed. Initially I was apprehensive as
I felt I would be in a vulnerable position. I questioned to what
extent the students would see my educational philosophy
demonstrated in practice.

However, this proved to be the most exciting and valuable part
of the initiative. I was for some students their group tutor, their
supervising tutor and the headteacher of the school. I could
observe them put into practice what they had been doing at
UWE and they could observe the way I taught and managed a
nursery school. I was also able to be involved in their reflections
in the sense that I could refer back to sessions at UWE or to a
particular reading to reinforce their experience. In this respect
their school experience was an extension of group tutorials
albeit in a different site of learning. Furthermore I was uniquely
placed to support them working on their assignments in school
and to help them engage in practical theorising.

The skills I was to deploy are essential for anyone who takes on
the responsibility for mentoring students in school. My partial
immersion in the culture of higher education had, however,
helped equip me for the role I was to play.

By acting as a role model and providing opportunities for students to
observe, try out and talk through the particular philosophy of the
school with regard to early years education, the teacher fellow provided those students placed with her with a rich resource to integrate
and advance their own learning. However as she herself commented:

It can be questioned whether it is an advantage or disadvantage
for a student to be in my school since it could be argued that
they are 'over exposed' to my educational philosophy in both
the university and in school and could reduce the possibility of
students developing their own philosophy. Since I am in a
position to assess both the students' practical classroom
competence as well as their written assignments, this could
leave them little scope to do other than emulate my values and
practice.

The fact that this experience for students was offset by two other
school experiences during their thirty-six weeks meant that what was
offered was in effect counterbalanced by that afforded by other
schools. The structure of the course ensured students had ample
opportunity to reflect, compare and formulate their own philosophy
and approach to early years teaching.
Nevertheless, the students supervised by Mary did not, during

this school experience, have access to input from any other university tutor since she was acting in a dual capacity. Although there was nothing to suggest that this was problematic for the students we are aware of research which suggests students find benefit in the separate perspectives given by teachers/heads and those of university tutors. The perspectives of the former tend to be coloured by the need for students to fit into and conform to the school's existing practices whereas the perspectives of the latter may be more student-centred encouraging students to engage in alternative approaches to progress their own development (Williams et al. 1992). It would be wrong to conclude from this that teachers in school are any less student-centred but rather to recognise that for teachers their primary responsibility is for the learning and development of their own pupils as students and they are likely to be unprepared to put this at risk even in the interests of securing any advance in the learning of those placed with them as student teachers.

Working with the student teachers in school was, however, only one aspect of Mary's role and she was encouraged to make other contributions to the course.

As a headteacher attending conferences and meetings with other headteachers and working with other professionals in the education system I was aware of expertise within these groups which could meet the needs of the students. Hence I was able to recommend guest speakers. I was able to provide skills and strategies for working with other professionals and parents, and contribute from my working knowledge of the implications of recent legislation such as The Children Act. I was also able to share with my colleagues at UWE all the literature received from the DFE and the LEA. The flow of information was not, however, one way since I in turn benefited from attending lectures given by leading researchers at UWE whose research findings I was able to share with my school staff and headteacher colleagues.

On another level, I was invited to talk to headteachers and teachers at a partnership meeting when they met students who would be completing a school experience in their schools. In this instance I was able to raise issues of a sensitive nature more easily than my UWE colleagues, raising their awareness of the importance of introducing students to children, staff and parents, furthering students' professional development by involving them in staff meetings, Inservice Days and PTA functions and allowing access to Curriculum Policy Statements.

It was therefore the specific expertise and contacts Mary had as a head which enriched the educational studies dimension of the course whilst her experience as a co-ordinator for science in her school enabled her to act as a catalyst for change in the early years science curriculum bringing together the depth of subject knowledge held by university staff with her own expertise. This complementarity of expertise between the partners was to benefit the students as evidenced in their ability to apply their learning more easily in their classroom practice.

In reviewing her various contributions to the course and hence to the students it is important not to lose sight of the professional development for staff, one of the Faculty's other precepts of partnership. Studies, for example McKenna (1990), have shown the benefits to individuals personally and professionally that participation in mentoring can make in terms of professional rejuvenation, in enhancing skills and increasing the capacity of all staff in partner schools to reflect on and analyse practice.

This is borne out by Mary's experience:

> The short term effect of my secondment was that staff in school took on wider roles and greater responsibility thereby enjoying personal and professional development opportunities from within their own work situation. The long term effect could mean career advancement for those who have gained experience they would not otherwise have had.

Additionally the students themselves had acted as catalysts for change since they had prompted re-examination of the rationale for existing practices within the school.

> During the spring term when there were four PGCE students plus myself taking part in school staff meetings, planning and review sessions produced this comment from one member of staff, 'We are having continuous in-service training in this school'. The school staff were coming to realise fully the positive input of the students and the influence of my continuing professional development in the university culture.

Whilst staff development benefits have been apparent for the school these have also been two-way with university staff benefiting from the curriculum and pedagogical expertise as well as a specific benefit emerging for Mary's mentor in the Faculty. He is to take on her role as head whilst she visits pre-school establishments in Sweden. This experience will be of particular relevance to her mentor, a tutor on a university management course, as the return to a headship, albeit briefly, will provide him with a reciprocal opportunity for professional updating.

The teacher fellowship pilot has therefore had benefits for both partners although it has raised a number of issues which our future partnership plans need to take into account and these include commitments of time and energy from all concerned.

Conclusion

The various dimensions of our existing partnership developments described here have evolved over time and been incremental in their effect of enabling us gradually to build stronger and more trusted working relationships, some of which have extended to include in-service activities in line with the precepts outlined earlier. This gradualist approach has also enabled us to begin to build up a picture of those schools whom we believe are fully conversant with and carry out the roles as currently agreed and designated. Furthermore, it is allowing us to identify those who are developing a commitment to a training culture within their schools for their own staff as well as students such as to enable us to feel confidence in their capacity to assume responsibilities for the extended training functions which will be required of them should they choose to be involved with us in the implementation of Circular 14/93.

Reflecting on some of the lessons we have learnt from our current approaches we are mindful of the training needs of schools. In particular we are aware of the longer and more sustained period of induction enjoyed by teacher fellows and the more limited mentor training we envisage being able to afford to offer teachers from all our partner schools when we implement the new circular. Furthermore it is difficult to envisage the assignment of mentors on the scale required. Our experience of designating Faculty staff as link tutors to act in such a capacity across a cluster of schools is a strategy we have adopted on our secondary PGCE school-based course. This could be an appropriate way to offer continuity of support from the Faculty as our primary teacher partners come to terms with the changes in their training roles and responsibilities. However the reduction in resource from the funding body to higher education institutions including our own is likely to make such support across schools increasingly difficult to maintain.

Equity of experience and provision have emerged as issues in our more conventional partnership arrangements. These will become necessarily much more difficult to guarantee when the responsibilities for delivery and assessment become shared by many more providers whose ethos and commitments will not all be well known to us nor necessarily inclined to support the principles of reflective pedagogy which we ourselves are committed to develop in our students. Without the necessary congruence of perspective between partners about the importance of critical enquiry students are likely to feel tension between the expectations of their university and school-based tutors. This may lead as Crozier et al. (1990) have suggested to the uncritical reproduction of classroom practices in order that students be judged by their schools as 'professional', conflict minimised and the partnership maintained.

To avoid such 'stasis' (Menter 1989) and to enable training which carries the hallmark of higher education that is 'the spirit of enquiry ... a willingness to listen to other points of view; and the freedom to question current orthodoxies' (Patten 1993) our school-based partners will need to recognise their role in jointly delivering higher education rather than just working with and supporting students during their time in school.

Changes of role and function will also be necessary for university tutors. Part of their role will need to include monitoring the execution of the responsibilities held by schools through more extended quality control and quality assurance procedures. These will be vital if we are to continue to honour our principle of students' entitlement to a high quality course in such dispersed and diverse settings.

Securing the number of partnership schools prepared to assume these more extensive training responsibilities and to enable our PGCE students to continue to have three contrasting experiences during their year we envisage being problematic. The factors referred to by HMI (DES 1991) namely the small size of many primary schools and the lack of non-contact time for teachers are likely to make it impossible for some of our existing schools to see themselves as having either the capacity or expertise to become more fully involved let alone assume full responsibility for training. In fact, on the basis of returns to the Faculty during consultation with our partner schools in response to the government's proposals for the training of primary teachers, 71 per cent of schools commented on the problems of providing effective support for students on the current arrangements even with considerable support from the Faculty (UWE 1993). The schools cited both the combination of National Curriculum requirements and their small size as contributing features. Whilst the former may well become reduced if the Interim Report on the National Curriculum and assessment (Dearing 1993) is indicative of future policy, this may well be insufficient to persuade others to become more fully involved unless they become part of a cluster of schools as advocated in 14/93. Such arrangements can, however, produce their own problems in terms of both the transfer and distribution of resources, management and quality assurance. These difficulties are likely to become more pronounced as it also becomes necessary to audit across the training sites the contribution of each partner to the curriculum and to the hours of directed time devoted to training in the teaching of the core subjects of mathematics, English and science. Such monitoring will inevitably become necessary as the time in the Faculty for the delivery of these is reduced.

We have referred to a number of issues to which we will need to attend in moving our PGCE more directly into line with Circular 14/93 and these will need to include a further review of which elements of training are best located where whilst retaining the integration to which we are committed and avoiding any split between theory and practice.

We began by referring to the challenges which face those involved in the training of postgraduate primary students. Those challenges are likely to increase in the near future as we learn to work in new and different ways with our partner schools. What remains essential in our work as teacher educators is that we provide high quality training for our graduate students and work to achieve this together through a complementary division of labour between ourselves and schools with an ethos of reflectivity and mutual trust.

It has been questioned elsewhere (Whitehead and Menter 1993) in the context of Circular 9/92 whether the secondary training policy thrust to partnership will lead to a reconstitution of the professionalism of participants as well as having an impact on the professionalism of new entrants to the profession. These will be equally important to monitor in the context of primary training.

Some of the practices described serve to exemplify what is possible as well as to remind us that partnership as lived out in practice has different meanings and consequences for those whose professional development and educational opportunities may be enhanced or impaired by such arrangements. Government policy directives and exhortations to partnership need to be fully cognisant of the complexities in territory as yet relatively uncharted. The stakes are high for all concerned.

4 The PGCE and the training of secondary teachers

Jenny Harrison and Cathy Gaunt

Setting the scene

Education at every level is undergoing change in the western world. With shifting values and changing economic circumstances, and with increased knowledge about how we teach and learn most effectively, these in turn have brought about redefinitions of the goals and the processes of teaching and learning. Teachers today need a wide range of skills to meet the increasing demands made upon them. They not only need to be committed and well-educated subject specialists, able to diagnose pupils' learning problems, but they also need to help pupils with personal difficulties, and to communicate effectively with parents, governors and the local community. Some teachers ultimately take on responsibilities of leadership in a particular curriculum area or take a share of the responsibility for the financial management of the school. There is clearly a need for effective training and learning throughout this professional life, and a crucial part is in the first year in initial teacher education.

Partnership should be viewed more widely than the obvious link between schools and the university department of education. It can be defined as a linked activity, with the most important factor in the equation being the trainee teachers, who bring with them a myriad of experiences and skills—many very relevant to teaching—which can be built upon, using many different starting points. Another factor in the partnership equation is the body of pupils in school. All our common efforts are directed in the end towards giving pupils a richer and more rewarding experience in school. Currently in Initial Teacher Education (ITE) secondary teacher educators are being asked to improve the quality of teaching in school (DFE Circular 9/92) to parallel the work done with trainee teachers. Certainly trainee teachers must be encouraged to concern themselves primarily with children's learning.

Trainee teachers need to realise that schools exist in communities and to be able to place the school in which they work in such contexts. Of course learning takes place in situations other than schools and is brought about by people other than teachers, and in places other than school and colleges. It is for this reason that facilities such as zoos, museums, libraries, art galleries, theatres and concert halls which all promote life-long learning, should be acknowledged for the part they play in the learning process. In ITE trainee teachers must be helped to recognise the value of experiences for their pupils which go beyond the classroom or laboratory, and may encompass the residential week, or work experience in an industrial placement. Some trainee teachers have personal experiences of field activities, notably on residential science or geography courses. Indeed there is clearly a place for all trainee teachers to gain such experiences and be involved in the negotiation, planning and management of such events. They could also be part of the briefing/ debriefing process of work experience with pupils, find out what pupils get out of the placements, or what teachers get out of such placements, and likewise what industry or business gets out of it! The crucial thing about these settings is the creation of specific goals for pupils so that the learning becomes more self-directed and has a particular significance.

Devising links with the community is part of the partnership, and linked activities can provide a greater understanding of other people's skills, styles of management, and better communication and a mutual regard for each other's efforts. Trainee teachers need to think critically about how their practice should take account of parents' perspectives, and an interesting project to enhance the trainee teacher-school-parent partnership is to be found in Hannon and Welsh (1993). Partnership, however, is more than a linked activity—it is clearly a joint commitment, involving time, effort and resources to a venture designed to produce joint benefits.

The needs of the trainee teachers

The first stage of the training process is to identify areas of personal need and develop confidence as a subject specialist, and subsequently to develop confidence as all-round professionals in classrooms and the school. To be successful therefore ITE has to provide a number of opportunities which can allow each trainee to:

- acquire basic teaching skills
- play a full part in the normal life of the school
- gain experience of working collaboratively with teachers to improve the quality of pupils' learning.

These have to be placed within the wider context of the life-long professional development of teachers and the process of school improvement. Trainee teachers need to be equipped with the power of self-evaluation, and the professional skills with which to carry this out. There is, therefore, a place for classroom evaluation and opportunity to develop the skills of a 'reflective practitioner'. The work done in Leicestershire in the 1980s on IT-INSET (Everton and Impey 1989) influenced the practice of many of the teachers, including headteachers, presently involved in the training.

The partnership model of training at the University of Leicester

This evolved over two years of a pilot phase and is currently in its third year of a fully-fledged programme. The partnership model at Leicester was already well-advanced when the requirement that schools should play a much larger part in ITE (Circular 9/92) was introduced. This has resulted in relatively minor changes to the time spent in school, shifting the proportion of school-based work from about 60 per cent to the required 66 per cent of the course. The structure of the course and the current arrangements for involving partnership schools in the overall programme are shown in Figure 4.1. Trainee teachers spend two days a week, when not on block

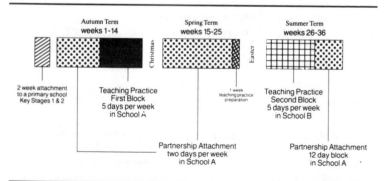

Figure 4.1   Current arrangements for involving partnership schools

teaching practice, in a particular cluster of partnership schools early in the autumn term followed by a block practice in one of the schools in the cluster. A further two days a week are spent in the school in the spring term (followed by a second block practice in a different school) with a return to the partnership cluster for the final three weeks in the second part of the summer term.

Currently fifty-one schools in Leicestershire and Northamptonshire are involved. They are grouped into seventeen clusters to provide experiences of the 11–18 age range. Typically in Leicester city a cluster may consist of two 11–16 schools and a sixth form college; in Leicestershire a cluster may be two 11–14 High schools and a 14–18 Upper school; in Northamptonshire there may be a collaboration of several 11–18 schools. About sixteen students are attached to each cluster, with between four and ten students from various subject specialisms, per school.

The underlying principles of the course

A holistic approach to ITE

It allows links to be made between subject specialisms and the wider dimensions of the teaching role. Figure 4.2 shows a sample arrangement of the two-day partnership attachment in school.

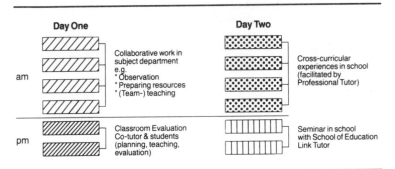

Figure 4.2   Sample arrangement of the two-day partnership attachment

Wherever possible students work as a pair attached to a subject department and work closely with a designated teacher (the co-tutor) forming a team of three. This team plans, teaches and discusses much of the work throughout the year. More particularly, early on, trainee teachers can work with small groups of pupils, and can both observe and be observed in a supportive atmosphere. The university subject tutor works closely with these school co-tutors to form a closely-related subject programme at the university.

As the year progresses the work of the subject team becomes more focused and more closely concerned with classroom evaluation. Examples of this will be described in the next section.

The second strand to the PGCE programme is the professional course which is a core of ten topics studied by everyone and is concerned with whole-school issues of relevance to all teachers regardless of subject specialism. It is intended that these two strands (subject work and professional course) should be experienced as part of an integral course. Whenever whole-school issues arise, links can be established between the two. Wider dimensions such as equal opportunities, special educational needs and personal and social education can be incorporated into subject work. This process is aided by the fact that currently the majority of university tutors have dual roles as subject tutors and professional course link tutors. Trainees spend an equivalent of one day per week on subject work and one day on whole-school issues.

All trainees are required to study these ten topics (see Figure 4.3); in school some are chosen for study in more depth because of student preference or as part of project work determined by the school to inform development planning in the school. There is considerable informal support here by the school's professional tutor in negotiating work by the trainees in different aspects of school life.

The teaching strategies adopted in the professional course are centred on a loose-leaved collection of materials on the professional topics. They require independence in study and promote links between university and school-based work. Presently trainee teachers have a weekly school-based seminar with the university link tutor in which professional course topics can be discussed within the school context. The teaching and learning styles in school include the following strategies:

- independent self-directed study, singly or in small groups
- group presentations
- progress tutorials with the university link tutor involving individual action planning.

Continuity of professional development

Individual action planning and target-setting have become an important part of the Leicester training. They involve negotiation by the trainee with tutors and peers in the university and likewise with teaching colleagues and peers in school. Given that one of the principles of partnership is addressing continuity of professional development from ITE through the early years in the profession to

1. **Positive discipline and good relationships in the classroom**
   class management; behaviour of groups; making sense of others' advice

2. **Promoting equal opportunities for all learners**
   for girls and boys; for different racial and cultural backgrounds

3. **An effective use of information technology**
   your skills on entry and on completing the PGCE programme

4. **Helping learners and assessing and recording their progress**
   the individual learner; groups of mixed ability and attainment; particular
   teaching/learning methods; principles of assessment and record keeping

5. **Whole school responsibilities in basic skills**
   teaching basic skills in all areas of the curriculum; information skills; language
   skills; provision for all children with special needs

6. **The cross-curricular themes of the National Curriculum**
   economic awareness; citizenship; environmental educational; health education;
   careers education and guidance

7. **The pastoral system and personal and social education**
   tutor group skills and responsibilities; your legal responsibilities; support
   services outside the school

8. **Links to other schools and colleges, and with the world of work**
   liaison and transition; 16+ entitlement; the world of work; European and
   international links

9. **The school and its community**
   the roles of parents and governors; activities involving the community;
   community education; the image of the school

10. **The education debate**
    the legal framework; evolution and structure of the education system; the
    origins of comprehensive schools; recent changes including the Education
    Reform Act; current issues including LMS, GMS; future controversies

Figure 4.3   Professional topics

positions of responsibility in a school, the process of target-setting underlies these assumptions of partnership. Not only is individual action planning a natural extension of this work, it also mirrors such work with pupils and students in many schools and colleges in which they are encouraged to take greater responsibility for recording their own achievements and for identifying and negotiating their own future pathways. Trainee teachers are thereby getting direct experience of action planning and direct involvement in the tutorial support from their university link tutor that is needed to make it succeed.

In summary

Partnership provides for joint planning between university and school, joint evaluation, and, indeed, has created opportunities for curriculum development for all the institutions concerned. The overall aim of the university/school partnership model is one which

provides benefits, in terms of professional development, to all participants: the trainee teachers, the qualified teachers, and the university tutors.

Implementation and analysis

The university perspective

I shall consider the development of good practice in ITE in my role
in the university, as science subject tutor and as link tutor. For a
university tutor, in both these roles, the main benefit is close and
sustained contact with a cluster of schools which provides recent and
relevant experience of current practice in a specialist subject as well
as whole school issues.

The trainee teachers are at the core of the training process, and
the graduates who join the PGCE secondary programme bring with
them an array of skills and experiences; some arrive straight from
undergraduate courses; more than half arrive with a variety of additional work-related experiences—of social work, nursing and
teaching, of research, of managerial work and industry, and many
others. To some extent the training process begins with their recruitment some months earlier, during a selection exercise which
occupies a full day and involves a visiting professional tutor. The
candidates have a chance to explore with their peers their particular
motives for coming into teaching, and to demonstrate their skills of
relating with people, their capacity to communicate, and their
understanding of the importance of their own curriculum area.
Though, presently, the final decision of acceptance rests with each
university subject tutor, it has been necessary and valuable to
involve teachers in the selection exercise. To some extent the
decision-making is shared; the teachers' insights are valued, and the
presence of the teachers at this crucial stage has been important for
sharing the quality of the applicants. The whole of the training year
is a filtering process, and always there are some recruits who realise,
or have to realise before completing the course, that teaching as a
career is not appropriate for them. The accumulation of evidence
and the counselling process associated with this is time-consuming
and has been largely the responsibility of the university tutor, sometimes supported by counselling services within the university.

Science subject work

In this partnership scheme you (*the trainees*) will have to take a
lot of the responsibility for your own learning, planning ahead
and building up records of what you have done.

This is an extract from page one of the *Science Handbook* for the science trainees (Leicestershire Partnership Scheme for Initial Teacher Training, Autumn 1993). The onus of responsibility on planning a way through the year is supported by the individual action planning process. The essence of this is to get trainee teachers to set manageable targets to be achieved within reasonable deadlines, and to accumulate evidence of competence according to the required CATE criteria (CATE 1992). The section headings for the science file: subject knowledge, subject application, class management, and assessment and recording progress, are used as the basis of trainee assessment in these areas and have been somewhat modified to include aspects of work that relate to science teaching. Thus laboratory safety, which is not documented in the CATE list, has been included and science trainees are expected to demonstrate a knowledge of the safety rules and the hazards in the laboratory, be able to organise equipment safely, and know their legal responsibilities, and the ways of dealing with accidents. This cannot be left to reach the trainee by a process of diffusion, and, in the future, co-tutors in schools may have to plan a clear training programme in this area, within the context of good departmental practice.

In my work as a science team tutor in the university dealing with up to twenty science graduates, my responsibility is to negotiate school placements and ensure continuity and coverage of the work; to read the plans and the materials that each trainee produces, to respond with guidance and suggestions and practical help with the next stage. We structure much of the science work in the university around a science team—a group of graduates of several different sciences, within which the trainee can explain the ideas of the specialism to a supportive but demanding audience. This enables tutors to address the first principle of partnership which is to explore links between subject specialisms and to consider the wider dimensions of the teaching role, including the exploration of a variety of teaching and learning styles.

Such a multitude of experiences in the various partnership schools allows for examination of the problems and insights during this university subject time. The trainees are in a position, as in an open science department in school, to learn from each other more about the in-depth knowledge and understanding of the subject. This can be a heavy agenda for some science graduates for there is an expectation in many schools for them to teach across three sciences to Key Stage 4 (Harrison and Pritchard 1992). At the university, subject tutors run a big variety of science workshops in which trainees can participate and broaden their base of subject knowledge and experience. In the future more of this work will have to be covered in school-based time. The difficulties of appropriate subject coverage, where individual needs can vary enormously, will be compounded in school once tutorial responsibility has been transferred to the science co-tutor. Not only will science co-tutors be helping trainees identify any weaknesses or gaps in science subject knowledge, they will be assisting also in providing ways of supporting specific subject needs.

At the university four science teams can come together—as a science 'superteam'—and benefit from the particular expertise of the contributing science tutor, thus covering areas such as information technology, health education, the use of language in science, and so on. The recruits receive a broad perspective of an issue, rather than one that is constrained by the boundaries of a particular school. They have opportunity to select reading, discuss and formulate their ideas in an environment which does not impose expectations of the working institution upon them. Will there be opportunity or time in school-based work for this to happen in a critical and unbiased way?

One of the important ways in which university science tutors have been able to maintain close active involvement in a school department is in the spring term, through a collaborative project, with a focus on pupils' learning. The aim of the work is to give everyone involved (experienced *and* trainee teachers) a chance to stand back from their normal teaching and try to enhance the learning and the learning environment of the pupils, and to involve everyone in some systematic observation and analysis for that purpose. Normally trainees are paired and work alongside a co-tutor, or another interested teacher. Projects are 'owned' by the science department, are part of the science department's development and they are carried out collaboratively. Past examples include:

- Monitoring pupils' oral presentations of project work
- Developing differentiated work in a science topic
- Devising and trying out a 'science town trail'
- Examining strategies for more discussion in science 'A' Level classes.

Trainees are required to present an oral report to the science department as well as a written report to the university science tutor, both to disseminate the work more widely and thereby involve more than just the co-tutor in the outcomes, and also to allow the department to provide feedback to the trainees, and consequently contribute to the final assessment of the project. In the future it is possible that the entire project might become the responsibility of the co-tutor, and the research and development opportunities provided by the university tutor involvement will be lost.

The benefit for the school co-tutors is the chance to explore evaluation techniques which can be linked to research into subject issues, or linked to work with subject departments in other schools, perhaps in the cluster. There is a chance to explore the relationship between subject area and the whole curriculum; and through overall involvement, an opportunity to develop management, interpersonal and tutorial skills.

In an attempt to identify some of the benefits of Partnership to science co-tutors and to science trainees, I circulated questionnaires to both audiences at the end of the autumn term (1991). Our early goals for the trainee teacher in school for the autumn term can be recognised as early competences and described as follows:

- Forming a good working relationship with the co-tutor and student partner
- Getting to know a class
- Doing a demonstration
- Discussion and preparing a safety issue
- Helping to organise a class practical
- Devising and evaluating a worksheet
- Monitoring pupils' work
- Discussing a topic plan in preparation for teaching practice.

Our task at that early stage had been to allow the co-tutors to engage with the raw or undeveloped teaching skills of a beginning teacher and to begin the process of sharing their own expertise in a structured way. We received feedback on a large variety of ways of working, ranging from:

made them join in ... delegated staff to do this deliberately

provided a booklet on systems and resources—they (*the trainees*) investigated the department for themselves

to

much discussion happened at lunch-times.

Perceived benefits for the co-tutors included items such as:

highlighted various weaknesses in departmental organisation

individual student teachers bring new ideas on a particular topic ... we have been able to stop and think about our own work ... discussions with students have highlighted thoughts that were in the back of our minds

having extra adults in the classroom gives the regular teacher

extra options in teaching . . . extra people give an interesting
change to the atmosphere.

Of course, too, we received comments on the costs to the department
in terms of time and general wear and tear. What was apparent was
the sheer diversity of experience for the science trainee teachers in
the thirty-four different schools, and it is this central issue which still
has to be addressed.

In a more recent attempt to identify the various *roles* of a science
co-tutor, I drew up the following list:

1. Providing a good role model of teaching in the subject area.

2. Guiding / counselling / advising / coaching / assisting trainees
   with planning their way through a structured PGCE
   programme.

3. Supporting (either directly or indirectly) the collaborative
   project.

4. Monitoring and assessing teaching practice.

5. Being a source of information about subject content,
   teaching methodology, and school procedures.

6. Providing a good departmental model with schemes of work
   for the National Curriculum, and providing access to a range
   of pupils and resources.

7. Removing any constraints and negotiating on behalf of the
   trainees with other teachers in the department.

8. Interpreting the CATE competences so they make sense to
   trainee science teachers.

These roles, in turn, raise questions about the range of skills needed
to be an effective co-tutor in any subject area. It is likely to be a
daunting list, and one in which there are tensions, for example, the
conflicting roles of 'supporter and enabler' and 'supervisor and
assessor'. Here are some of the *skills* and *experiences* I believe are
needed to be effective as a co-tutor or university tutor in science:

- Previous and recent teaching experience of at least three
  years

- Up-to-date subject knowledge and expertise

- Ability to demonstrate a variety of subject teaching methods
  and to enable others to use them

- Knowledge of assessment and evaluation, including self-
  assessment

- Active interest in own professional development

- Interpersonal skills necessary for the provision of tutorial support
- Awareness of the needs of the trainees at different stages of the PGCE year
- Ability to identify good classroom practice
- Provision of structured guidance within a framework of observation/ analysis/ reflection
- Ability to work collaboratively in teams
- Good communication skills
- Ability to organise one's own time as well as that of others
- Awareness of equal opportunities.

In the current political climate it seems, as a university subject tutor, I am systematically writing and talking my way out of a job at the university, to enable co-tutors in schools in the future to take over most of the aspects of the subject training mentioned above. In other words co-tutors in schools—with minimal time and no opportunity to gain a broader overview of a variety of school settings—will endeavour to deliver the same training. Nevertheless joint work done in developing a science handbook for trainees to support their school-based work, has been enhanced by the formation of a science development group of teachers and university science tutors. Some of the difficulties in delivery of school-based training have been identified, and the production of support materials for the trainees, with suggestions for tutorial strategies and within a common framework of expectation and delivery, has been started. This is an area in which ongoing support from the university, in the delivery of necessary professional skills through structured INSET or co-tutor training, can continue. True partnership is clearly an active process. It is about offering teachers, and indeed all participants, an opportunity to develop a broad range of professional skills.

Professional course work

The ten topics shown in Figure 4.3 form the framework for the coverage of the professional course which spans both university and school-based work for the trainees. The topics can be matched to some extent with the CATE competences listed in section 2.6, 'Further Professional Development' (CATE 1992). Discrepancies do occur: for example, two components, information technology, and the Education debate, both feature strongly and separately in the Leicester Professional Course.

There have been good examples of joint planning and delivery of seminar sessions in school, which draw on the special expertise of school staff in areas such as special needs or Records of Achievement. University staff can provide the focus for discussion and debate as well as taking charge of the assessment of this part of the course. For the school professional tutor contacts with trainee teachers and their group work provides opportunity for identification of specific curriculum and staff development needs in certain subject areas, or broader areas of concern to the whole school. As with subject work, the current concerns of the school will to some extent determine the professional course topics which are studied in depth by each trainee. There is regular contact too with other professional tutors and the university link tutor, which can increase awareness of the work of a wide variety of staff. Finally through overall involvement in the partnership there is development for the professional tutor in terms of the professional skills of co-ordination, management and good interpersonal relationships.

At the time of writing it is likely that in the near future schools will take charge of providing the coverage of the professional course components of the course, and possibly its assessment. Professional tutors in school will be called upon to provide tutorial time to the trainees for the professional components of the training programme; the support materials will need updating and revising; and the delegations that will result will depend as much upon the outcomes of the financial and contractual arrangements as upon the best rationale for training.

The concept of continuity of professional development which forms the second underlying principle of partnership provides an approach particularly appropriate to ITE because of the variety of strengths and experiences which different people bring to the understanding and skills that are needed in a teaching career. It is therefore important to begin what is effectively the planning of further professional development, and to use a process which will be encountered later in appraisal schemes. The use of individual action planning and short and long term target setting with associated tutorial support from the university link tutor means the trainee teachers are getting practice in the articulation of their skills and in identifying in a constructive way areas of specific need. They can begin to set achievable goals and gain practice in listening, clarifying and summarising, giving and receiving feedback, being assertive, and so on. Likewise appraisal is involved with the asking of questions, making observations in the classroom and sharing good practice with colleagues.

Certainly partnership has begun to demonstrate ways in which improved ITE for trainees can go hand-in-hand with authentic professional development for teachers and can contribute to a school's programme of curriculum review and classroom evaluation. To quote Newsom in the *Time Educational Supplement* (13 November 1992), what is assumed is:

> that the institutions each have a well thought-out development plan of which professional development of staff is an element; and that in such circumstances, the initial training becomes part of a continuum of professional and institutional development.

For the university tutor, with either link or subject hat in place, there is close and sustained contact with a cluster of schools which provides recent and relevant experience of subject and whole school issues; there is the possibility of developing parts of the PGCE course in response to developments in schools as well as being pro-active in these developments. There is also a place for the university tutor in the delivery of aspects of necessary professional skills through *structured* INSET in schools—an example, has been a contribution to 'in-house' sessions on appraisal. Finally and importantly, in such partnerships, it is vital that all the opportunities for development and research work are retained.

The school perspective

The exciting benefits of trainee teachers working collaboratively with practising teachers were first seen at Uppingham Community College in 1987 when a group of PGCE (Secondary) trainee teachers joined teachers in the college and tutors from Leicester University School of Education in an IT-INSET programme researching into group work and its effects on pupils' learning. For further details of IT-INSET work see the first section of this chapter, and Everton and Impey (1989). The enthusiasm generated during this short-term exercise inspired both the teachers in the school and the tutors at the university to embark on the early stages of the partnership scheme of school-based training; this scheme has developed rapidly over the subsequent years and contribution to teacher training is now an established part of the curriculum and research programmes at Uppingham Community College.

The principal strength of school-based teacher training is in the immediate and extended exposure of trainee teachers to the realities of life in school. After only two weeks of university-based induction trainees are sent out to partnership schools and are faced with learning a whole new culture from a fresh perspective—that of a teacher. It is the responsibility of the professional tutor to ensure that trainee teachers experience induction programmes which both inform and support the first phase in their chosen career.

At Uppingham the first morning is spent mainly with the professional tutor but includes a tour of the college led by pupils. Some formal dissemination of information is balanced with more informal discussion of school ethos, routines, partnership principles and the year ahead. Trainees spend the first afternoon in subject departments with their co-tutors and most of the time leading up to first teaching practice is spent with the co-tutor and professional tutor in preparation for the intimidating prospect of an initial teaching practice. Preparation includes observation of classes and teaching styles within the department, gathering of resources, planning lessons, working with small groups, discussion of departmental policy and team-teaching.

The co-tutor, in collaboration with the subject department, plays a key role in the nurturing and training of a trainee. The co-tutor is not necessarily the head of department but should be an experienced teacher who is skilful in sharing his or her experience with a newcomer to the profession. The co-tutor is responsible for:

- arranging sessions of subject-based observation which cover a range of approaches, content, year groups, abilities etc.
- discussion of observations
- preparing the teaching practice in negotiation with the trainee and other subject staff
- team-teaching with the trainee
- observing lessons led by the trainee, taking notes and discussing the observations
- supporting the trainee in all aspects of the subject-based work
- ensuring that the trainee feels a part of the departmental team.

The first teaching practice is a daunting experience for many trainee teachers but induction activities prepare them well for their first attempts at class management. They are given the opportunity to work with classes before teaching practice actually begins and to team-teach with the regular class teacher to lead them into schemes of work, which they, themselves, may be delivering. Although they are not forced into total responsibility for a class or classes before they are ready, the majority are keen to be allowed to 'go it alone' from the beginning. The co-tutor remains close at hand in case an emergency should arise.

A successful school-based induction programme will result in a less stressful teaching practice, as trainees will feel comfortable with the routines of the school and the department before having to cope with the realities of class teaching. They are observed on a regular basis by the co-tutor and other members of the department and at least three formal observations are recorded during the six-week practice. The co-tutor and trainee meet regularly to discuss lesson plans, strategies, problems and successes, and the trainee is also supported by the whole departmental team and by the professional tutor. Certainly at Uppingham this type of support network has built up a security for trainees and has reduced the feeling of isolation which beset so many training teachers in the past.

It is during the spring term at Uppingham that most of the exciting collaborative work takes place and it is then that the school really gains from the input of teachers new to the profession. At Uppingham we have built up a culture of research and development which informs a lot of the teaching and learning taking place. Each year new research projects have emerged through one or more of the following routes:

- targets detailed in the college development plan
- HMI recommendations
- consultation with all staff
- consultation with trainee teachers
- new initiatives, either imposed or voluntarily adopted.

Research relies heavily on data-gathering through classroom observation, interviews, questionnaires, video and audio tapes, investigation into schemes of work, strategy statements, and so on. Trainee teachers and experienced teachers working collaboratively in evaluating current practices provide a powerful and inspiring mechanism for informing change and development. One of the projects worked on by a team of practising teachers in collaboration with students focused on the provision available at the time for pupils in the college with special needs. It was recognised that the remedial programmes for pupils with learning difficulties were, in some cases, inadequate and the desire in school was to re-structure the support offered. Data were gathered through observation, shadowing of pupils with learning difficulties, interviews with staff and students, visits to other schools, working with the LEA Special Needs Service, through evaluation of resources, of different strategies (such as in-class support or extraction) and of rooming. Trainee teachers were involved in every aspect of the research carried out. Following the collection of all the information a development plan was drawn up for the establishment of a curriculum support department with adequate staffing, funding and its own well-resourced and comfortably furnished room. As a direct result of the research and findings the principal and governors agreed to the proposals; the curriculum support department was launched and it now provides an extensive and flexible programme of support to pupils who experience learning difficulties both in the long and short-term.

The benefits of a project of this nature for the college are obvious, but the trainees also gained an enormous amount of experience through watching youngsters learn, observing a range of teachers in action, raising their awareness regarding learning difficulties and influencing a school's development. This is only one example from a series of partnership projects which have involved trainees; other projects have included:

- an evaluation of college library facilities which led to the development of the library as a resource centre with open access to all users

- the college link review (phases 1 and 2) investigating the provision made for more able pupils.

Link review was a process initiated by Leicestershire Education Authority in 1992. Embedded in the national climate of evaluation and review, each school and college within the county embarked on a short-term review focusing on a particular issue linked to each institution's development. County link officers worked with teachers in schools on investigation, research, evaluation and subsequent amendments to and developments of current practice.

There is no doubt that a very real *partnership* which has existed between trainee teachers and practising teachers has been a productive relationship not only in terms of training some excellent practitioners, but also in informing some significant developments in the college's recent history.

One of the strengths of a successful school-based teacher training programme lies in the confidence and flexibility of the teachers in schools. Experienced practitioners should not only be able to share useful strategies and techniques but also be ready to recognise other equally successful ideas offered by colleagues new to the profession. At Uppingham, where there exists a fertile climate for initiative and development, trainees have been welcomed as a vital resource in creative terms.

For school-based teacher training to work well it must be at the heart of a school's development and feature in the development plan. At Uppingham the college development plan is a working document underpinning all the work carried out by departments, support staff and management teams. Both departmental and whole college targets are highlighted in the development plan and the trainees link in with these targets, either through their work in departments or through their research into cross-curricular issues. The college development plan itemises all the INSET needs of teams and individuals within the college, which in turn informs the financial planning. It should be pointed out that creative usage of the INSET budget has supported aspects of the teacher training programme at Uppingham, as the current limited budget of £500 per student would not adequately fund the quality of programme offered at the college.

In order to release the professional tutor on a weekly basis, time has been plumbed-in to the timetable at an early stage and regular supply staff have been employed on short-term contracts. This has allowed not only the professional tutor to work with trainees but also with other staff at appropriate stages during the year. During the link review, and other larger-scale projects, whole teams of staff were released for one morning each week to collaborate with trainees on issues directly relevant both to the needs and development of the college and to the professional course of the PGCE programme.

The most significant and valuable aspect of school-based teacher training is the opportunity for trainees to sample real life in schools today. This experience develops as the year progresses and trainees find themselves increasingly in situations faced by qualified teachers on a daily basis. At the beginning of the year the thought of taking an unknown form's register at twenty seconds' notice would send the majority of inexperienced trainees hurrying for refuge in a seldom-used store-room. With familiarity and a six-week teaching practice behind them, trainees become more confident and more ready to offer their services in solving some of the minor crises which occur regularly in most schools. An ability to take the initiative and a willingness to be flexible are two qualities which are added benefits to school-based teacher-training.

Trainee teachers usually develop a sense of belonging to the college to which they are attached and consequently feel part of the day-to-day routines. They are seen from the outset as members of staff; they are provided with lockers, a pigeon hole, staff handbooks and all the other fringe benefits enjoyed by regular members of staff. As the year progresses and their experience widens it becomes possible to involve them in an increasing variety of situations. It is critical, however, that schools do not merely make use of trainees as a source of free supply teaching. This type of exercise would negate the spirit of partnership which should be a mutually beneficial relationship, whose principal aim is to train and prepare trainee teachers for a career in teaching.

Not only does the training package prepare trainees for delivery of their subject but also there is considerable emphasis on the pastoral side of school life. Trainee teachers are well-informed with respect to the theory of personal and social issues, but the realities of working with groups of pupils on sensitive topics or counselling individuals can only be learned through experience. It is only possible to provide a sample of a range of pastoral work during the year but this gives trainee teachers a firm foundation on which to build.

Attachment to a tutor group, usually that of the co-tutor or another member of the department, gives the trainee a daily contact with a tutor group, and teaches skills necessary to administering pastoral business—taking a register, reading notices, checking appearance, chasing up absences, etc. Trainees also attend assemblies, form tutorials and, when appropriate, counselling sessions—all of which provide at least a taste of the pastoral aspects of a teacher's role.

Final teaching practice, in a school other than the original partnership school, occupies a large portion of the summer term and gives trainees the opportunity to consolidate the strategies and techniques acquired during the autumn and spring terms. Trainees take on a greater percentage of teaching time and more significant responsibility for all aspects of teaching and managing a class. Co-tutors are able to devolve more responsibility to them and to be more exacting in their requirements of professional standards, for example, more thorough assessment; a stricter regime for setting and marking homework; more creative lesson planning. Trainees on final teaching practice will have been in partnership with a different school and consequently will require an induction programme during their teaching practice preparation week.

The closing stages of the partnership year form the least structured part of the whole programme. Trainees are expected to return to their original partnership schools for a period of two and a half weeks. During that time they will be involved in at least some of the following activities:

- teaching classes with whom they have already worked
- team-teaching
- experimenting with new strategies learned on final teaching practice
- departmental planning for the following year
- resource building
- end of year college-based activities programme
- a limited amount of supply cover
- project work.

This section of the partnership programme can be disrupted by the trainee teachers' natural preoccupation with seeking employment. Either they are called for job interviews at this time, or, if they have already been fortunate in securing a post, they are anxious to visit the new schools and familiarise themselves with new routines, learn timetables and begin planning. Professional tutors need to be flexible over the arrangements they have made. Although the majority of trainees feel a sense of loyalty and continuing commitment to their partnership school, they are keen to prepare fully for their first teaching appointment.

The partnership school can also benefit from the programme in terms of recruitment: last year at Uppingham Community College we appointed one of our four students to an English post. There were advantages in this appointment both for the school and for the newly-qualified teacher. The school appointed a candidate whom they already knew could cope with the demands of the job and who worked well with the departmental team. The newly qualified teacher was familiar with the school culture, routines, staff and so on, and consequently did not have to master new systems and procedures as well as grapple with demands of a first teaching appointment. The school-based induction and training led logically into the supportive programme for NQTs and consequently there was a consistency in term of target-setting and monitoring. As school-based training in all institutions becomes more uniform, through closer collaboration and sharing of good practice, NQT programmes could all follow a similar logical progression, ensuring that teachers in their first and subsequent appointments receive more support and guidance.

Trainee teachers are valued as full members of staff at Uppingham Community College. They are welcomed into the college, supported in an intensive and varied programme of training activities and involved in all aspects of school life. Without their presence and the support of the university link tutor and university subject tutors a lot of the exciting and productive research which has taken place during the last five years, would have been considerably reduced in its scope and effect.

Evaluation and pointers for the future

University tutors have, as the focus of their work in ITE, the trainee teachers recruited to train in their institution. In terms of the university tutors' own professional work in this area the quality of the training process has always been a priority and it is one that is firmly embedded in a theoretical framework.

School tutors have, as their first responsibility, the teaching of the pupils in their care. The involvement with the trainee teacher, especially during teaching practice, has been one traditionally which parallels the relationship between master craftsman and apprentice.

Tutorial support has been provided often on a 'as need arises' basis. The 'craft activities' of teaching can be located in some of the headings of the CATE competences list: most particularly with respect to *class management, assessing and recording pupil progress* and some elements of *subject knowledge and application.*

The shift in emphasis that is occurring in ITE is to place some of the onus of responsibility for the *quality of teaching and learning in schools* on the training process itself. In other words teachers are required to manage many more aspects of the training process than the 'craft activities'; university tutors are required to play a lesser role, and to train the school tutors to take up aspects of assessment and tutorial work with the trainees, as well as to relinquish the opportunities for consideration of the broader educational issues in both subject and professional areas.

It is clear from the partnership work, in which we have been involved, that there is a symbiotic relationship between university tutors and school tutors: it is a relationship which requires both partners to cooperate and contribute in order for it to be mutually beneficial. University tutors need the reality of classrooms and pupils in which to place the broader ideas in context; school tutors need expertise from people with the time and opportunity for research, development and critical reflection of the broader issues. This model goes far beyond the 'craft activity' model of training, for it is in this way, we believe, that the quality of learning and teaching in schools can be enhanced.

Our partnership work has benefited in the past, firstly from injection of money from LEA (for the IT-INSET work), and subsequently from the school itself. In an institution where the presence of trainee teachers is not seen as an added burden to the responsibilities of teachers, but instead is perceived as a contributory factor in the school's programme of review and development, partnership work in ITE provides a vehicle, for example, for the trainee teacher to demonstrate 'the self-critical approach to diagnosing and evaluating pupils' learning' (CATE competence 2.6.7). It remains to be seen whether similar collaborative work can continue with the new funding arrangements. Proposed new arrangements for school-based funding should not, in fact, jeopardise the future of school evaluation and development work. However, it should be recognised that without the input and support of the university tutors, the success of any school-based research is likely to be minimised, and only by buying back the support of the university tutor will the mutual benefits for school and university tutors be retained.

In the future a major concern will be the issue of quality control. Keeping in alignment the developments and approaches to training in different subject areas is already a headache for the university.

Once much of the training agenda is passed over to professional tutors or subject departments in schools, what will be the commonly agreed expectations of any one tutor? How will their work be monitored? The report of the external consultant at the University of Leicester (July 1993) reflected on the evidence of good practice concerning the professional course. Generally speaking a more cohesive experience was gained by trainees where professional tutors were able to take part in the planning (with the university link tutor) of the joint seminar in school, and to forge links with other aspects of school life. The professional course handbook, with its extensive resource materials, was not being used consistently by all professional tutors. Only about 30 per cent of schools were currently offering structured school-based professional course work. Clearly there is an important area of training need for professional tutors: to understand the competences required by trainee teachers, and to participate fully in the organisation of a professional course which is firmly embedded in the good practice of the school. The mutual advantages which result from the careful collaboration of the teachers in school and the trainee teachers, supported by the university tutors, can lead to research and development, and positive change in the school. It is these important outcomes which have to be disseminated in the training process.

Similar concerns affect the subject-based work in training. As there evolves a shift in the overall responsibility for assessment of subject work to the co-tutor in school, the need for consistency in expectation of the minimum standards expected of a newly trained teacher have to be spelled out. No-one has yet identified what qualities are needed to be a 'good subject teacher'. It is crucial that levels of competence are identified at all levels of professional development, so the training with the new recruits fits into a pattern of continuing professional development. Only then will the trainees be able to identify their needs, set their own agendas and embark on a professional training towards competence.

In examining some of our fears during the change to more school-based courses, the speed of the transfer is of concern. Too rapid a transfer of responsibilities is likely to lead to loss of goodwill of the schools, and a demise of the partnership which has been built up. The quality of the training will be diminished as the level of individual tutorial support for each trainee is greatly reduced. Faced with the transfer of resources into schools it has to be recognised that university tutors will be deployed elsewhere, and the coherence of the present programme will not be maintained, despite the efforts of all the partners to provide high quality training. There will continue to be a place for a link person to be assigned to a group of schools, to provide both a university perspective and a school perspective to the training programme. This would go some way to merging responsibilities for the oversight of all aspects of the training delivered in that group of schools. There is now a requirement to comply with Circular 9/92; we have to accept the probability of loss of quality training, and attempt to provide structures which will minimise the likely reduction in quality.

5 Undergraduate teacher education for primary teachers

Mike Cornish, Alison Hamer and Beatrice Reed

Introduction: general and local background

As outlined in Chapter 1, the character of the BEd degree for the primary age range roused high feeling and vigorous debate during the 1980s. The issues often reflected divisions between teacher educators themselves, between priorities in teacher education units and schools, as well as concern over the Government's stipulations through Circular 3/84 (DES 1984). For example, how sharp a difference should there be between preparation for early years (3–7) and later years (7–11)? How central and immovable was the role of the 'across-curriculum' class teacher? How (relatively) important was a holistic approach to children's learning in comparison with understanding secondary/GCE-type subjects?

Such issues—and many others from the mid 1980s—remain prominently with us in the 1990s sharpened, if not necessarily invigorated, by the messy flood of demands though the National Curriculum and by government pressures for new kinds of priorities in teacher education: most obviously to do with the enhanced role expected of schools, but also to an extent (confusingly) undermining 1980s' stipulations concerning the prominence of specialist academic subject study for all primary age range teachers.

These past ten or more years have been stirring times throughout education and the University of Northumbria (still known more comfortably in local schools as Newcastle Poly) was deeply engaged from the early 1980s in the tensions created by being instructed to abandon what was one of a handful of innovative four-year BEd degrees built around the multi-subject role of the class teacher and the centrality of a structured sequence of school experiences tightly linked to specific aspects of professional preparation. One of the toughest consequential tasks was to hold on to the strongly professional ethos while incorporating the Government's main course recipe for the decade—quality through two years of specialist academic study. Our chapter concentrates on this strand of activity. We address initially some of the issues encountered—both 'theoretical-ideological' and practical—and then concentrate on how the course process and outcomes evolved and are still evolving. Our dominant focus is on one core curriculum subject—English—but with wider references and general implications where this seems appropriate.

Making professional sense of specialist subject studies

Arguments concerning the nature and extent of subject study appropriate for primary teacher trainees can be heard within the ITT world and spread their focus in many directions outside formal teacher education, e.g. university subject departments, child development specialists, early years education groups, curriculum developers for (especially small) primary schools, and—latterly—National Curriculum designers. The establishment of UPTEC (evolving into NAPTEC—(see glossary) and its consequent activities and publications (NAPTEC) illustrated one line of response to a 'felt need' among many teacher educators; while such texts as Morrison's (1989) and McNamara's (1991) raise both practical and conceptual 'subject competence' in North American schooling and teacher education.

In our own local context we have wanted to 'make stick' a number of stances:

(a) A degree designated to prepare primary teachers should provide specialist subject study which supports this central purpose: e.g. many, if not most, familiar BA English literature studies components do not meet this need as well as other kinds of emphasis in English studies.

(b) The studies and activities associated with classroom practice in a given subject study should be as demanding and important in assessment terms as any other aspects of subject study; and if possible should be transparently informed by these other aspects.

(c) In order to move towards the potential role of subject co-ordinator in a school, students should gain experience in the complexities of understanding school-wide subject policy and practice in the culture of a primary school, and should also underpin their contribution to subject's potential development in schools by engaging with practical enquiry-based learning in support of that subject.

(d) Students should associate progress in their HE-based subject study with related work in school throughout their programmes: e.g. a key area such as early literacy should be informed not just by (inevitable) attention among many other priorities during full time block periods in school, but also by structured attention in more limited spans of time.

(e) During their final period in schools, leading to assessment for qualified teacher status, students should be in a position to demonstrate their quality as specialists and part of their assessment profile should reflect this. Similarly a substantial focus of the final period of their four-year programme should constitute an independent extended study, with a view to strengthening insight into their specialism.

Each of these intentions brings a problem or two—whether conceptual or practical: e.g. In relation to (a) the paradigms of different subjects in 'respectable' education do not lend themselves equally straightforwardly to tailoring study towards primary students' needs. In relations to (b) and (c) the traditions of many primary schools do not easily create space for this kind of attention—though the arrival of the National Curriculum (in its current form, at least) raises the stakes for reviewing such traditions. In relation to (d) and (e) the number of variables associated with student placements for block periods, the untidiness of annual shifts of staff, and curriculum priorities or initiatives in schools, and the number of schools needing to be worked with for year cohorts of 120 plus (and up to 300 in some HEIs)—all these may combine to frustrate the best laid plans.

Picking up pieces of partnership

So far this sub-section has implied, rather than explicitly addressed, the importance of co-operative relationships with schools. Long before the Government's discovery (and then immediate destabilising) of 'partnership' as a key priority for effective initial teacher education, many courses were posited on close co-operation at least with a proportion of schools offering placements for trainees. The contribution to this of the Council For National Academic Awards validation and review policy and practice in the 1980s can hardly be overestimated: HEIs were increasingly required to articulate and demonstrate their relationships with schools, usually including opportunity for CNAA of private dialogue with teachers and students. Though clearly 'selected old pals' in validation contexts can provide a tokenistic side-stepping of serious and complex co-operation on a wide scale, many genuine efforts were made to reduce the stereotypical dichotomies of theory–practice, ivory tower–real world, and academic–professional.

At Newcastle Poly moves from *ad hoc* areas of co-operation towards more elaborate partnership for the purposes of primary subject specialisms have not been part of a systematic grand plan. The initial priority—articulated in the early 1980s at a time when it was necessary to explain the concept of 'serial school experience' to HMI as well as to headteachers—was to find contexts of subject-specific good practice at infant and at junior levels which were also capable of 'absorbing' significant numbers of students in ways which were mutually useful: and to do this without the (to us untenable) expense of the current IT-INSET model. This led to different characteristics for school-based provision across the four subject specialist areas offered: the range of 'confident' contexts available for science and technology was (predictably) much smaller than for maths and English, and this led to a narrower spread of contexts and student experience in the former than the latter.

Similar untidiness can be found in the engagement with ITT since the mid 1980s of a number of teacher-tutors who took on responsibility, within their own schools, for virtually all the supervision and assessment of one or more students during one of the block periods spent in school: though there was structured preparation and annual review/updating of arrangements, virtually no attention was paid to discussing a student's specialism and matching this to the kind of experience likely to be available through the teacher-tutor.

However untidy these (and other) co-operative activities, they nevertheless laid the ground for much organic networking, which made more feasible the examples of collaboration analysed in the main section of this chapter.

Commentary on recent practice

This section will review in some detail arrangements to enhance, through partnership, the quality of the English specialism from the point of view of university tutor and teacher in school, with a commentary from students. (We have not been ambitious enough to engage children as learners in contributing to current judgements.) This review will then be set alongside a briefer set of observations on other concurrent collaborative efforts to try to draw out some of the key positive and negative features to be managed.

The university perspective

In this account I will outline how and why partnership activities with teachers have become an integral part of the experience of students taking the English specialism of the four-year BEd at the University of Northumbia. At this university students specialise from the end of their first year. Virtually all teaching is done by a small core team of tutors for each specialism who take responsibility for academic and professional studies and their associated serial school experience.

The current degree has been running for six years and within the English team we have found that the intensive and extensive involvement that we have in the students' education over three years has provided a context for initiatives which link across professional, academic and school-based work. This would not, perhaps, have been the case in a more fragmented programme. A major focus of initiatives for the English team has been enhancing the opportunities students have of working with teachers on projects which are significant and beneficial to both parties.

These partnership activities have evolved in two ways. First, and for the most part, they have concerned the manner in which the five English serial school experiences are structured. Secondly, they have been built into course work. In both cases the developments are ongoing and the advantages of working in partnership are increasingly evident. Importantly, students gain confidence and a more indepth understanding of their subject and of the complexities of being a teacher or subject co-ordinator. Equally, we have found that teachers are more willing to work with us when they see their involvement in terms of reciprocity.

Diversity in partnership activities

The school-based enquiry programme

(see glossary at end of chapter for working definitions of selected terms)

A key principle of the four-year BEd is the development of students as reflective practitioners. A feature of the realisation of this is that students are taught approaches to, and techniques for, undertaking research or enquiry in schools. They are involved in enquiry projects during their third and fourth years Within the English specialism, this aspect of the course has been the strongest vehicle for the development of partnership activities.

The initial move towards partnership took place four years ago. It involved fourth year English specialists and primary English co-ordinators. At the time I was supporting both groups in undertaking school-based research projects: the former for extended independent studies, the latter as part of their MEd degree and an LEA action research project. It became clear that there were considerable overlaps in the work being undertaken by both groups in relation to the issues emerging from their research and the problems they faced in carrying it out, and that each could benefit from the other's perspectives. As a result students and teachers worked and took part in sessions at two full day research workshops at a teachers' centre in the LEA.

The two workshops revealed not only that teachers and students could work together as equals, but also that they could learn from and with each other. For both groups it was evident that a considerable shift in how they perceived each other took place. For the teachers this arose from their surprise at the extent of students' knowledge of both research and the teaching of English and at their ability to articulate it. For the students, their perceptions of 'self' in relation to teachers altered: first, they became aware of teachers as learners as opposed to the 'all knowing'; secondly, they gained a greater sense of, and confidence in, their own knowledge. The workshops also revealed that despite the teachers having had students from the course on placements they had very little knowledge of, and thus had not been able to take advantage of, the education that students had in both specialist and other areas.

From the above initial partnership activity a set of guidelines began to emerge. These underpin, and have continued to develop with, each of the subsequent partnership activities. They are:

(i)   that any projects undertaken have to be 'real', to contribute in some way to curriculum or professional development within the schools involved and to the education of the students

(ii)   that teachers need to be informed about what the students have done and what they can bring to projects

(iii)   that (ii) can be achieved most effectively by working with teachers who are already familiar with the work of the university e.g. past BEd students, MEd students or those contributing to teaching on the BEd

(iv) that tutors have to be opportunistic, in terms of maintaining an awareness of development activities taking place in the schools they work with, capitalising on these to create contexts for partnership projects where the varied needs of school and course can be met

(v) that teachers need to be made aware of the work we do with the intention that they will approach us in the future

(vi) that the optimum arrangement is cyclical, whereby tutors learn from the work of the students and teachers and use this knowledge to modify and enhance the courses they teach on.

As is apparent from the above list the passing of information between all those involved in partnership activities is seen as critical to their success. For our part as tutors, a main concern is that there is a shared understanding of what is going to happen, why it is going to happen and what outcomes are envisaged. The success of the serial school experiences, to which the discussion now turns, is reliant on this.

As a result of the workshops, attention was directed to enhancing students' serial school placements through re-focusing them towards partnership based models. The first move took place again as part of the School Based Enquiry Programme, this time in the third year of the students' course.

By the beginning of their third year students have completed two block school experiences alongside a substantial amount of serial school experience. In this, they have gained experience of preparing and planning work for children, but have had no extensive opportunity to observe and reflect on broader issues to do with the practice and policy of teaching English in a busy primary school.

Prior to the re-focusing towards partnership, students had been involved in a serial school experience designed to offer the opportunity for such reflection. Then, as now, the experience was built around two aspects of their specialist study:

(i) cross-curricular issues, within the professional English programme

(ii) the introduction to methods of classroom enquiry programme.

For the purposes of the experience students design and carry out a small-scale investigation for which the broad focus is language and learning as part of a cross-curricular issue. Initially, these studies focused on things which appeared interesting to the students, and whilst teachers were aware of what was happening the studies were not necessarily related to issues significant to them. This had a number of disadvantages, crucially the projects lacked reality, and although they provided a sound vehicle for developing research techniques, they often afforded a somewhat superficial perspective of the subjects investigated. Alongside this, students felt that they lacked direction and that they were just being 'fitted in' according to who was willing to have them.

For the past two years, although the structure of the programme has remained the same, the studies have taken a different form. The exact focus of each study is now directly linked to curriculum development projects in the schools taking part in the serial school experience. In order to achieve this, the process for 'selecting' the schools has undergone a substantial transformation. This no longer takes place on the basis of who will be willing to accommodate the students' needs, but rather, where there are teachers who feel students can make a contribution to the work of the school through their studies. This year, for a cohort of thirty students, there were five schools involved. Two of the schools have headteachers who are students, working with me, in the university's MEd in Educational Development, and who are undertaking their own school based enquiries; in the third school students are working with past English specialists now in their second year of teaching, and the final two schools are part of the Newcastle Inner City Literacy Project and have worked with us for some time. The number of students in each school is dictated by the nature of the project they will be working on; they tend to work in pairs or fours within groups of six or eight aligned to an age phase of their choice.

During the summer term prior to the experience in the autumn, negotiations take place to establish the foci for the projects and to make clear how the students can work with the teachers.

The foci for this year were varied, for example:

(i) In an early years unit, how is language used in the role play areas, what kinds of language are used and what prompts this? How could the areas be adapted to enhance language use?

(ii) In years two and six of one school, in what ways do children gain access to words to support their writing, what influences the choices they make and what effects does this appear to have on their attitude to writing?

A third example can be found later within this section where the contributing headteacher details her school's perspective of being involved in this serial experience.

This year the students were in school for six half days, with an initial half day as a preliminary visit. Each year students negotiate with teachers over what data-collection techniques would be most appropriate to satisfying the research interest. In general these take the form of participant observation, interview and questionnaire, however, video and photographic evidence has also been collected. The timing of the half days, with deference to the students' time-tables, is also negotiated in relation to the needs of the project. Tutors take an advisory or consultative role as it does not seem sensible to spend time observing students in activities of this kind, rather to support them in shaping their projects with the teachers. At the end of the experience students write up a report of insights emerging from their studies and, where appropriate, tentative suggestions for action.

This partnership activity, involving students in working with teachers on mutually beneficial projects, has afforded a number of advantages over the previous model for this serial school experience. These build on and extend the advantages already identified in relation to the research workshops discussed above. They are that students can:

(i)   see teaching in a broader context

(ii) gain insights into curriculum-development and school-development plans

(iii) see themselves as professionals making a contributing to the work of professionals

(iv) through being placed in a position of responsibility, be enabled to take more independent responsibility for their work

(v)   gain insights into the real role of reflection and evaluation in schools and classrooms

(vi) achieve a greater awareness of how school staffs can work.

(Following this account will be students' perspectives of working with teachers in the manner described.)

As was mentioned earlier, in the fourth year of their course, students undertake an extended independent study into an aspect of English. These studies are school-based and draw on both the students' academic and professional programmes. Through the re-focusing of the enquiry project outlined above to embrace partner-ship so, subsequently, the nature of these extended studies has also begun to change. Whereas in the past students tended to do research on an aspect of English now they are working with teachers and, for example, advisors on studies which are significant to the people involved. Many students have increased confidence in approaching people and negotiating over their projects. They are keen to make them worthwhile, and are also more sensitive to the political and social constraints which must be considered when working in any institution.

The writing workshop serial school experience

This SSE takes place in the third term of the students' second year. The students spend this term of their professional English programme studying the teaching, acquisition and assessment of writing. Alongside this they are, as part of their academic programme, writing and learning techniques for writing at their own level. The purpose of the SSE is to involve students in writing projects that are already underway or just beginning in schools.

An important feature of the SSE is that the work students do with the children should not be isolated to the half-days when they are in school, but should be integral to writing going on at other times with the class teacher. Equally, it is necessary for students to have a clear focus for their planning and of how this will contribute to the overall development of the projects at hand. To facilitate the above it is necessary for, initially tutors and teachers, and then students, tutors and teachers to plan together.

Topics typical to this SSE include:

(i)   writing a school newspaper or magazine

(ii) writing books of poetry

(iii) writing books for younger children

(iv) literature-based writing activities in the early years.

Schools who work with us during this SSE tend to have been closely involved with the National Oracy or Writing Projects or part of Language in the National Curriculum. Past English specialists in their first and second year of teaching have also taken part. In this way we are familiar with their work and they with ours.

Although this SSE focuses on writing and supporting its development, the advantages for students outlined earlier in relation to the Partnership in Enquiry Programme hold true here. Students are engaged in 'real' projects and involved in working closely with teachers. As a result they gain more confidence in themselves as teachers and more knowledge of how teachers work.

For tutors a key advantage of working on SSEs such as the two described is that we learn a great deal more about what is actually going on in schools. This has implications for the content and shape of the programme we run for students and, in turn, because we are more aware of schools' needs, of the way we can address continuing professional development for teachers.

The teaching in multilingual classrooms project

This activity takes place in the third year of the course. Its purpose is to give English specialist insight into, and experience of, how to plan effectively to meet the needs of children, who have a first language other than English. To this end, we have worked closely with one school over the past four years. The project takes place in the school on two afternoons. These visits replace the professional English sessions the students would have had at the university. On the first afternoon students are introduced, by teachers, to the philosophy, policy and practice of the school; they see round the school and talk with children about their work. In addition, they have the opportunity to study and discuss curriculum plans for each school year group. At the end of the afternoon the students are given the topics which will form the basis of the work in each year group during the following term.

Over the next week groups of four or five students per year group develop these topics into language-related schemes of work; in keeping with the philosophy, policy and practice of the school. The development of these topics continues when the students return to the school the next week, when they discuss their ideas with the teachers. We have attempted to consolidate the experience for the students by establishing a peer tutoring activity where they take sessions with non-English specialists focusing on teaching in multilingual classrooms.

Partnership activities can, as I have detailed, enhance the education of students in initial training in a number of ways. Probably the most significant concerns students' involvement in their own learning. Where partnerships are at their most effective, and students and teachers work and learn together, students take a far more active role and develop a much stronger commitment to both their work in schools and in the university. Alongside this the nature of the projects means that there is a far greater chance of congruency between the activities which take place in the two locations. Thus students see the work in the university as more relevant to what goes on in schools. I consider a measure of the success of the projects to be the number of students who now seek to return to their SSE placements for the Block School Experience (BSE), negotiating with schools and liaison tutors to achieve this. This has implications for broadening the base of subject-specific partnership activities from serial to block experiences to be discussed later in the chapter.

The students' perspective

The students, whose voices have been recorded in this section, were
fourth year English specialists. Their comments were part of a group
interview in which they agreed to take part for the purposes of this
chapter.

Although I have classified their comments into five areas relating
to their perspective of partnership activities with schools, I have left
the students to speak for themselves.

1. The advantages of partnership

> Often on school experience the teachers just walk out of the
> classroom, this was completely different, then you're not
> learning anything from them and they are not gaining anything
> from you. This time they were still doing their jobs and we
> learnt from each other.

> If there is a partnership, while you are not in school on SSE the
> teacher can carry on that sort of work, and when you go in it's
> been going on and that makes it more useful to everyone.

> You feel like you're doing a 'real' job not just being allowed in.

2. The importance of schools being informed and involved

> Schools need to be very aware of what we can offer.

> It would be better if the schools approached the college rather
> than college approaching schools because where the teachers
> aren't really involved in the project its not like partnership.

3. How students see the activities as useful to teachers and how
the students perceive their role

> The specialism allows you to make more sense of the data you
> are collecting. A lot of the teachers weren't English specialists
> themselves and they got a new perspective.

> In my class, the teacher pointed out things that she had noticed
> which gave me things to look at, at the same time I would tell
> her what I had seen. We co-operated.

> It was valuable to the teacher 'cos they don't often have a
> chance to stand back—it could motivate them to change things,
> we could swap roles.

4. Key advantages to students

Having a chance to work with teachers lets you know more
about schools, you get to see students' and teacher's view point
as well as your own and discuss ideas with other people's input.

By doing these SSEs you learn more about other aspects of
teaching than teaching.

Through writing the report (for schools) we were really made
aware of the knowledge we knew.

5. Ideas for development of partnership

The schools need to know what we have done, that needs to be
part of BSE.

Extend the notion of observation time in BSE, have it as time to
develop work in partnership with the teacher, to really build on
things children have done.

If you are an English specialist it would be really useful to work
with the co-ordinator for your specialism for at least one later
experience.

These comments, I feel, demonstrate that the students saw partnership activities as worthwhile. They felt that their experience of being
in school had additional value when they were working with teachers
and alongside this, they saw themselves as having more value
because they were making a contribution. In my opinion, at least
part of the students feeling that they had something to offer to
schools was engendered through their having engaged in partnership
activities with teachers. It is also apparent that the students felt that
they had been able to see teaching in a broader context, in fact the
kind of context in which they will eventually work.

The students interviewed were clearly aware that the activities
they took part in only worked when there were shared goals and
expectations. This highlights the need for thorough negotiations
between tutors and teachers both before and during the students'
time in school. It also, given the small scale of the English specialist
activities, underlines the administrative and communicative complexities which would accompany the desirable move of extending
partnership activities of this kind to BSE.

The students themselves seem to put forward a very useful
suggestion for extending partnership work into BSE through developing the opportunities for negotiation between students, university
and teachers prior to BSE. In this way, they felt, that a better match

could be made between their developing plans in keeping with the needs of the children to be taught. Through this the BSE could become more worthwhile to all those involved.

The school perspective

In this section I am going to provide my personal commentary as a headteacher on involvement with the university English section's school-based enquiry and the effect that this had upon my school.

As the staff team of a large inner city primary school we have been involved in the initial training of students on block placement for many years. We have also worked closely with the University of Northumbria in refining the role of teacher-tutors, through an initiative associated with students in schools on their second year block experience, and referred to in the following subsection more fully. This intiative was welcomed by the teachers who were given training in the teacher-tutor role. Staff felt involved in the initiative and were committed to producing quality training for students on placement. However, it is only since my involvement with the school-based enquiry project that I have begun to examine the role of student placement within the development framework of the management structure of the school. Our involvement in the Serial School Experience has given us a greater insight into the professional development within the subject specialism and the importance of giving students the opportunity of demonstrating such specialist skills within their block placement.

My involvement in the MEd course at the university provided a critical platform for the analysis and evaluation of current practices within the management structure of my school. As a recently merged infant and junior school our first whole-school staff initiative was to look at the developing ethos of our school. Staff invested considerable time and effort in drawing up codes of behaviour and lists of classroom expectations, and in discussing ways of ensuring these values were communicated to children, parents and governors of the school. The critical element in the process was how to engage the children in the process and give them the opportunity to discuss the values of the school, the values of the playground and their own personal value system.

The English specialists embarking upon their school-based enquiry project provided us with the resources to evaluate the effectiveness of our behaviour policy and monitor the developments taking place within the school. The Serial School Experience enabled us to use the skills and expertise of eight third year language students over a period of six weeks. The research topic was generated by the school and linked to a current major development within the school: thus, the students' school-based enquiry provided a real context for looking at how methods of classroom enquiry can be used to bring about change. The project placed great emphasis on collaboration between the students, the staff, the tutor and the school community. The observations, data and evidence collected by the students were used to review some of the ongoing developments within school to improve the quality of interaction in the playground during playtime and lunchtime.

The framework for the project was negotiated between the school, the tutor and the students themselves. Their involvement within this component gave them an opportunity to gain insight into the levels and power of communication channels within school cultures. The school in return would have the opportunity of using the students' research to learn more about the way in which our shared ethos binds a mixed community together. The students interviewed the children in the yard during playtime and lunchtime. The information collected in the yard was analysed and followed up by interviews in school, the data collected was then shared between the student group and the school. The focus of each session was negotiated from the analysis of the evidence collected. I was impressed by the students' insight into and sensitivity to issues raised and the professional way they conducted the enquiry. The students identified the need to involve other members of the school community and went on to interview the dinner assistants. Evidence was collected through taped interviews, field notes, photographs and video recording. The amount of data collected and the variety of sources gave us a unique opportunity to examine the staff value system, the children's value system and their interpretation of our 'shared' vision. The report prepared by the students will be used as part of a school-based review and presented to the governing body.

Within the context of the SSE students were given the opportunity of working alongside teachers as colleagues. The students' role as professional 'enquirers' gave them the opportunity to examine the external forces which often impinge on the day to day management of the classroom situation.

> I was able to see the school as a whole rather than just a classroom.

Often, students on placement in schools are under enormous pressure to perform in the classroom and are not given the time and opportunity to see how a school functions as a whole. Time spent in school as 'observers' gives students an insight into how a school functions, the roles and responsibilities of the head and curriculum co-ordinators. The students valued the opportunity to talk to the staff as professional colleagues rather than as students on placement.

> This situation allows you to converse with staff as a
> professional, it builds up your self-confidence in the staffroom.

Engaging in our school-based enquiry gave the students the opportunity to demonstrate their knowledge and understanding of their specialism within a real context of learning.

> I was able to communicate with curriculum specialists and share
> expertise. There was a sense of real purpose knowing that what
> we were doing is valued.

The comments from the students were collected during a discussion about the nature of the developing relationship between the students and the school. Students felt part of the school and some requested the opportunity to come and do a third year block placement in the school. Their reasons were valid. The school culture and ethos were known and valued by the students. They had already made contact with the staff in school and had the opportunity to establish a relationship with the children. They had knowledge of the day-to-day organisation of the school and access to the philosophy of the developments in process. All these factors would help the students plan more effectively for their Block School Experience. To facilitate this, contact had to be made to tutors involved in student placements and the partnership network increased.

Obviously, the success of a project like this depends upon the commitment of all parties concerned and a clear understanding of goals. But other factors also need to be considered:

- Time needs to be allocated to the staff involved in organising and co-ordinating the project to give them the opportunity to discuss the evidence collected. The time spent organising and planning the project is critical, all partners are expected to participate in defining the focus, methods of gathering evidence and the code of ethics.

- The university tutor needs time to help the students monitor and develop the initiative and by supporting the students in the process of enquiry they are also supporting the school.

- The project has to be based within the school's own development programme. Teachers knew that the work undertaken by the students was an essential part of the school review and valued their contribution. The students themselves felt that their work was valued and their efforts had helped support the school development.

The partnership between school, students and tutor was developed through negotiation and acknowledgement of mutual benefits to all parties concerned. The gains to the school, the students and the university in terms of professional focus contribute to a celebration of shared expertise and a sense of collegiality. We believe that our involvement with the SSE project raised teachers' self-esteem. The data collected provided evidence that what was taught in the classroom has had an effect on the way in which the children respond and behave in the playground. A further development from the SSE is that several members of staff have indicated that they would like to take part in a school-based enquiry project related to their own classroom practice. Our partnership with the tutors involved in the SSE had enabled us to establish a school-based programme to look at research methods suitable to classroom enquiry and my deputy head is now working with the research materials provided by the students to complete a module within the MEd programme, based on his own enquiry project.

As a headteacher I am aware of the need to support the idea of training teachers with a bias towards specialism. In my school, responsibility for the curriculum is delegated to curriculum co-ordinators who lead curriculum teams. Everyone is required to be a member of one curriculum team, most volunteer to belong to two. Today the need for Newly Qualified Teachers prepared to meet the demands of the classroom is paralleled by the need for them to be able to play an active part in working as part of a collaborative team and yet I have never considered a student's specialist subject to be a criterion for placing them with a particular class or year group. The distribution of students in my school has been left up to volunteers. We now intend to explore the extent to which we can build the SSE English components into planning future initiatives and how student placements can become part of the school's future development plan. In management meetings it was suggested that students in year 3 and year 4 of the BEd should be placed with curriculum co-ordinators following their particular specialism. This would enable students to examine the role of the curriculum co-ordinator at first hand and attend curriculum meetings. The students could contribute to the curriculum teams by discussing any current innovations supported by the tutors within their specialism. It was decided that the monitoring of students should be written into the job descriptions of all curriculum co-ordinators. To enable this initiative to work we need the co-operation of the placement tutor at the University of Northumbria. The contract between us would be of mutual benefit as we would be able to plan developments in curriculum areas around student teacher placements. In the development plan we have identified the role of mentor as a training need for *all* staff within the management training programme.

In the current climate of external pressures to provide school-based enquiry and evaluation, the need to establish closer links between schools and ITT establishments is essential. A partnership model of training between school and ITT would draw on the strength of both establishments recognising the distinctiveness of their respective contribution. As headteachers struggle to find the resources to fund innovation, the opportunity to access and use teachers' expertise and specialist knowledge should be exploited. Could other sections provide the support we need in return for the sharing of our expertise? We are building a reputation for providing quality training for students and staff. The link with the university is providing new challenges to help us prepare our new school to meet the demands of the 1990s.

Some broader aspects of collaboration

It should be evident from the preceding commentary that the activities were assisted by the relative simplicity of arrangements: a small number of university staff from a single specialist team, maximum informal interaction with school staff, minimum bureaucracy, and sharpness of focus across quite short periods of time. Though this favourable context did not prevent limitations emerging, it offered—and continues to offer—an impressively creative platform for continuing development.

Nevertheless, even in this context it was noted towards the end of the commentary that little, if any, attention was being paid to the relationship between *serial* experience and the more complex *block* periods in schools—either by the school as a valuable *locus* for curriculum specialisms or by the university as initial articulator of priorities, inter-relationships of course components, and progression across these over a programme whose formal 'pivot' was school experience. It may, therefore, be salutary briefly to set broader processes of collaboration alongside our main focus: hopefully, this will contribute to a more complex review in our final section when addressing positive prospects and challenging difficulties.

The traditional model of practical preparation for teaching (i.e. full time block periods each spent in a single school) engages whole year groups of students spread across scores of schools, perhaps several LEAs, and strikingly different catchment contexts. The model has been the focus for many initiatives which are concerned with HEI-school collaboration over the past decade—desirably so, since at a minimum any moves which reduce the lottery-like character of placements are likely to help enhance not just equity but also the quality of students' learning experiences.

The most recent primary age range initiative at this university has evolved from the late 1980s, when a range of schools were interested and willing to increase their supervisory and assessing role, supported by substantial textual guidance, but much more limited interactive preparation. More recently this relatively loose set of arrangements was re-shaped with a view to achieving a more coherent and genuinely negotiating team of teacher-tutors and university tutors working to agreed priorities. Supported by a small Enterprise in Higher Education grant at its preparation and review stages, the project concentrated on schools taking responsibility for the operational management of a full (second year BEd) block period. Some 50 schools, 10 university staff, and 100 students were involved, the scheme being seen as a further step towards more fully structured partnership in this aspect of undergraduate ITT, not least in so far as direct resourcing for the schools' operational role came from unfilled posts in the university's salaried entitlement.

The scheme implicitly or explicitly addressed some familiarly untidy features by the following procedures:

- engaging an appropriate and manageable range of schools through a preliminary conference and follow up initiatives
- identifying perceived key priorities of teachers to be addressed during preparation
- using and clarifying vocabulary with minimum ambiguities and maximum agreement on interpretation
- providing (with a view to refining) a set of supportive packages each geared to a significant feature of the teacher tutor role: such features having been identified by the teacher-tutors themselves as their main priority concerns
- preparing for the role in a collaborative way, based on quite small clusters of schools, which are each in principle supported by individual members of a university core team of tutors, who also contribute to moderating
- attempting effective moderating across schools by teacher-tutors themselves rather than simply by university staff
- providing a strong framework for post-block evaluative review on the part of students, teacher-tutors and university staff.

It is not part of the central purpose of the section to analyse in detail

this (still evolving) episode of collaboration in block school placement—it worked well in the eyes of the vast majority of each set of
participants, and for many provided a much more coherent and
cohesive model for early professional preparation than conven-
tionally supervised ITT. In particular, and among other positive
features, the vast majority of students regarded the kind of relationship available through a teacher-tutor based full time in school to be
particularly valuable in achieving detailed progress on areas of low
confidence such as meeting individual needs and effective classroom
groupings. (Alongside this many teacher-tutors found their more
structured and elaborated role with students increased their non
attenders to self-reflective professional development.)

However, notwithstanding the useful procedures adopted, and in
contrast with the sharply focused and more quickly shared and
clarified purposes of the specialist subject initiative, there were predictable inadequacies which derive essentially and cumulatively
from the number of *variables* involved across people and contexts (a
perennial issue regularly debated in ITT), from the *resourcing and
workload* pressures (a steadily increasing issue through the 1980s),
and from the *instabilities* of current schooling (perhaps a significantly
new 'psychological' aspect of the 1990s).

Such interferences with effective development are not confined
to primary education but are arguably especially complex to manage
where many schools are relatively small, where the historical staffing
base is narrow in its 'serious' subject expertise, and where the class
teacher role is strongly established in tension with some National
Curriculum demands. In short, this initiative took some small but
valuable steps towards qualitative improvements in partnership, but
in doing so reinforced the importance of being sensitive to the many
compromises to be addressed as an integral feature of any relatively
'bulky' collaboration in the educational circumstances of the 1990s.

In parallel with the issues emerging from a 'block' initiative, we
can also observe two further complications, which resist a fully tidy
and coherent solution to preparing for specialist competence as such:
both of these add to the agenda for future improvements. First, we
have indicated above that English is a long established high status
part of the primary curriculum in so far as it addresses the development of literacy and oracy. Also, as a subject, substantial areas of
academic content, most notably in language study, can easily be seen
to generate understandings relevant to classroom practice and children's learning. These features are less self-evidently present in
many other primary curriculum subjects. In our local situation, this
had led to subjects adopting different and not necessarily mutually
consistent approaches to collaborating with schools in preparing for
their specialism. For example, expressive arts specialists work

largely, as a full cohort group, in one or two schools with a particularly strong commitment to arts in education. In the case of science, only a very small number of schools has felt able to offer sufficient underpinning conceptual confidence across different strands of primary science. This has created much greater difficulty in balancing evenly and consistently the kind of understanding being attempted in the university programme with strongly established curriculum experience in school.

Secondly, and perhaps more importantly for long-term effective specialist preparation, we have to date concentrated our attention to specialisms on serial experiences. Though our objectives for each of the four BEd block experiences are consciously 'progressive' in expectations, the variables across placements and supervisor expertise have resulted in minimal focus on the evolution of each student's specialism through each block; or at best an erratic set of outcomes at the end of the final block across the student year group. It is interesting to note that the quite carefully developed teacher-tutor initiative described earlier in this sub-section barely raised the topic of specialism: at the middle of Year 2 stage, this presumably did not figure high on anyone's agenda in comparison with more obvious 'class teacher' priorities.

These brief resumes of other development work make it pertinent to distinguish within developments those aspects which are not easily generalisable and those which offer useful pointers for teacher preparation more widely. The final section of the chapter will concentrate on ways forward, while also noting what is likely to be problematic for the foreseeable future.

Pointers and challenges

In this final section we concentrate on three sets of implications from the rest of the chapter, utilising also some of the current trends in educational policy and practice. Again the major focus will be on specialist study, though there will be wider implications arising from some points and we will explicitly extend the perspectives where this seems appropriate.

Pointers for the immediate future

Capitalising on potential of serial school experience model

From the school's point of view, participating in this form of SSE is perceived as having direct and identifiable benefit for the school, as distinct from a task which springs solely from the needs of initial teacher training. Activities undertaken derive from agreed needs in the school: teachers knew that the work undertaken by the students was an essential part of the school review and valued their contribution. Moreover, in the case outlined, the mini-project also raised teachers' self-esteem. The data collected provided evidence that what was taught in the classroom is having an effect on the way the children respond in the playground.

From the university's point of view, students perceived their work to be valued by the school both in the short-term and in contributing to thinking about school development. They also were beginning to gain crucial experience in a positive climate of the way theoretically grounded school-based enquiry might operate; and they were doing so through activity which depended on their specialism, but had obvious broader educational ramifications for the evolution of the school. University staff were able to engage supportively in preparing students for enquiry-based methodology on a manageable scale and as a basis for more ambitious future work in the course, without the logistics being awkwardly expensive on staff time.

What is now needed is a more fully structured interaction between the key strands of the university's professional applications component of each specialism and associated small-scale but valuable development needs in schools: most realistically where schools are committed to SSE as a feature of ITT needing to be sustained and further developed within the expectations of Government approved 'school-based' training. Such a move could offer far greater potential for achieving consistency between the work planned by students and the ongoing work of the school—with benefits to all participants.

In the light of Government pressures to emphasise school-based minimum competences at the expense of more elaborate and complex preparation, it is especially timely to demonstrate a workable and valued set of arrangements which make substantial involvement of students and their HEI-base a highly valued feature of school development, through critically reflective enquiry. To achieve this, one of our own priority tasks is to 'audit' best SSE practices, and to interrelate such an audit with the evolution of enhanced school role for block periods. Such an approach offers an organically evolving approach to meeting the requirements of school-based training, though whether there is sufficient time available for such complex dialogue in the schedules needing to be worked to is another matter. Equally if we fail to do so, would not the meeting of needs take place at such a superficial level that the quality of the experiences, and thus their durability, would be questionable?

Strengthening attention to specialisms in later block practices

One of the outcomes of the initiative described earlier was the extent
to which students—over quite a limited timescale—come to feel a
genuine member of the school. Several, consequently, saw it as
sensible and logical to envisage pursuing one of their remaining two
block practices in the school. Their reasons were strong ones (unless
it is felt that 'deep end' unawareness is a necessary feature of all
blocks): they had a platform of familiarity to build from, and even if
they were to be deliberately 'placed' in a less familiar part of the
school than they had become used to, they would be able to 'hit the
ground running' in a way that is impossible for the conventional
block situation.

Whatever the issues of logistics and equity (across a large year
group) that this raises, it prompted much sharper attention in the
school towards the management of students' specialist needs during
block practice. For example, the school management team came to
see it as important to associate each block placement student with
the co-ordinating teacher for their specialism: students would be
able to examine the co-ordinating role at first hand, would be easily
able to attend relevant curriculum meetings, would know that preparation, practice and evaluation for their specialism would be being
overseen by someone with day-to-day concern for good practice in
the specialism. Moreover, students' initiatives could be fed into a
supportive and informed context; their 'strength' would not be seen
as something relatively marginal in the school. A logical and usefully
broadening consequence of this way of thinking is to incorporate
monitoring of student specialisms into the agreed role of co-
ordinators, as part of the school's greater explicitness and self awareness of their role in initial training.

Longer-term issues

Interrelating ITT, induction and continuing professional development

An earlier section illustrated the way in which third year BEd
students were able to work with, as well as for, experienced serving
teachers in enhancing provision for English as a specialism. It is
unrealistic to anticipate a thoroughly tidy and seamless flow from
specialist development in ITT through the induction period into the
second or third year of teaching: the variables in ITT patterns and
the variety of history, context and size found in primary schools
make for a very ragged situation on the ground. However, the grad-
ual clarification of National Curriculum expectations and the press-

ure on schools to address capability in specific subjects in a much
more direct way create a much stronger opportunity than, say, five
years ago, for identifying the induction period as a key to consolidat-
ing the potential specialism of students from more accelerated modes
of professional preparation. It is not unthinkable for this to be in
part achieved by engaging inductees in the kind of ITT activities
outlined earlier. Indeed in the past 7–8 years, where BEd routes
have paid serious attention to increasing the rigour and substance of
professional aspects of specialisms, there is a clear benefit in the
contribution which the final components of ITT provision can make
to INSET for some new teachers and many who were prepared less
fully in this respect.

More completely, a proportion of teachers with strong specialist
interests now sees great value in focusing their undergraduate professional development study towards the evolution of their specialism in terms both of its optimum character across the ITT stage and
of its effective implementation in different school contexts. Though
such an emphasis is likely to be confined to relatively small numbers,
its local influence could be considerable through the context of a
large MEd programme and through the contribution made via the
MEd into the ITT programme itself.

Cost-benefit implications for university and schools

Government policy is pressing all partners in ITT towards much
greater concentration on cash-linked relationships. To an extent
both higher education and schools are paying the price (literally and
metaphorically) for inadequacy in negotiating and articulating the
role of schools in ITT across decades of interaction, not to mention
the real staffing costs of the training process as a whole. However, we
can equally note the absurdity of being too exclusively cash and
school cost driven. It is self evident in the models described earlier
that not merely is there mutual student, tutor and staff development
entailed in the SSE model, but that in many respects the benefits to
the school are evident in a more reliable and predictable way than in
the more complex conventions and demands of individualised block
practices.

While it may be possible to devise imaginative ways through this
challenge if HEIs are given some flexibility in their use of numbers,
it is dismaying to encounter such incoherence and destruction at
such a fundamental phase of state education.

Erosion of evolving partnership modes

This chapter has illustrated a number of highly valued developments
springing from a process which roots the 'core' responsibility for

specialist preparation in the university but which engages university and school staff, and also students, in a collaboration focused on shared tasks to meet the needs of children's learning. Such collaboration on a wide scale is complex but promises progress of a quite new kind, in comparison with interactive relationships of 10–12 years ago.

All contributors to this chapter find it acutely disappointing, not to say destructively irrelevant, to find that Government policy now encourages the kind of ITT which in effect undermines the role of the university and diminishes the depth of academic study and professional enquiry which is currently possible. The implications of establishing a Teacher Training Agency are taken up elsewhere in this book. But we wish to emphasise, from the kind of primary perspective taken up in this chapter, that all participants in the activities described see the role of a higher education unit specialising in the full spectrum of teacher education to be essential for the continuing development of primary education.

The chapter therefore ends on this problematic note. Important partnership initiatives have been taken, and short and medium term agenda of a challenging but highly stimulating kind lie ahead. Yet the prospects are increasingly threatened by Government policy—in our context, distinctively characterized by failure (or refusal?) to acknowledge the demands and significance of early childhood education. At the time of writing our most important task is to achieve sufficient local cohesion to minimise this threat: a task which has to be addressed through national groups as well, but which in the end will only be managed successfully by achieving trusted and valued local structures which 'deliver' reliably.

Glossary

The following are working definitions used within the Northumbria University degree programmes and the text of this chapter.

Reflective practitioner   someone who is developing and transforming their practice through ongoing critical analysis and reflection on the practice itself.

School-based enquiry   investigations which are undertaken by teachers and/or students in the schools in which they work. It involves the collection and interpretation of data for the purpose of gaining a greater understanding of practice or other aspects of school life.

Action research   one of the ways in which reflective practice can be carried out. In this context it refers to an ongoing process through which teachers identify areas for improvement or development within their practices. It is based on collection and interpretation of data, leading to provisional action steps which are subsequently the subject of further review.

Serial school experience (SSE)   sequences of time spent in school on the basis of half or one day per week, normally with a small number of negotiated objectives linked to specific tasks.

UPTEC: Undergraduate Primary Teacher Education Conference.

NAPTEC: National Primary Teacher Education Conference.

6 Bachelor of Education degrees for secondary teachers

Julian Elliott, Carol Park and
Maurice Holliday

Moving towards partnership

The School of Education at Sunderland University has a well-established tradition of two and four year Bachelor of Education (BEd) degrees in what are largely shortage subjects, mathematics, science, technology, modern foreign languages, music and business education. These degrees have traditionally followed the usual pattern—the aquisition of subject knowledge together with teaching studies inputs intertwined with periods in school consisting of serial practice, where small groups of students work together in a classroom for one morning or afternoon per week for 6–8 weeks, and various types of block teaching practice. Other school-based experiences are also provided, for example, the two and four year business education students support teachers in a local school in its week-long operation of an experience-based learning programme (n.b. throughout this chapter the term 'school' is used as a generic term for all education settings catering for children aged between 11–18 years, middle and secondary schools, sixth form and further education colleges).

The four year BEd portfolio consists of two subject areas, design and technology and business education. Unlike many initial teacher education courses, these programmes do not largely recruit from the 18-year-old school leaver age range but instead contain a significant

number of students in the 25–40 age range who have been employed
in business and industry. Both courses focus on appropriate subject
knowledge (studied in both the School of Education and other university departments) and offer a range of practical school and industrial placements. Business education students, for example, not only
undertake the more traditional serial and block teaching practices,
they also undertake a fieldwork placement in a business setting.

The business field placement takes the form of a research project
agreed between the student and the host organisation, and provides
him or her with an opportunity to apply subject knowledge to a
professional context. Those students who came to the university
straight from school gain valuable business experience, while those
with a business or industry background, receive an opportunity to
broaden, update, and/or reassess their knowledge and skills. Similarly, the design and technology course provides students with an
opportunity to work with a business or industry in producing arte-
facts and systems through a major design project.

The two year BEd is actually one course, with students electing
to specialise in any one of six different subject strands (business
education, design and technology, maths, modern foreign languages, music and science). Although students study their own subject in specialist groupings, education and teaching studies inputs
are delivered in generic groupings, which provide students with
opportunities to gain a rather wider perspective of the teacher's role.
As is noted below, however, the heavy emphasis upon subject
specialism has, to some extent, led to insufficient consideration of
the teacher's wider role. With the advent of greater partnership with
schools, a more appropriate balance has been achieved.

The notion of partnership, although expanded by recent Government initiatives, has always been a feature of many higher education
institutions' relationships with schools. At Sunderland, this has been
particularly true in matters of course development and monitoring
and teachers and college lecturers have long been valued members of
course development teams and university validation events.

At the beginning of the 1990s, a series of developments paved the
way for the revised and more fundamental partnership currently
operating with schools. Modern foreign languages was added to the
two year BEd portfolio. Students received subject tuition in the
university's modern languages department and teachers from local
schools were paid, not only to supervise school placements, but also
to devise and teach the university-based subject application sessions.
Direct tuition by schoolteacher subject specialists, representing a
fundamental shift from traditional practice, is likely to become an
increasing feature as our subject profile broadens to accommodate a
greater number of National Curriculum subjects.

In 1992, a PGCE programme was introduced for the first time, initially in business education. This widening of the university's portfolio increased the number of school placements required and led us to reconsider what we meant by the term 'partnership'. The Government's apparent desire to increase the proportion of time students spent in school was, of course, a significant influence on our thinking although we were concerned to retain those features of our BEd programmes which had been recognised as 'good' and in some cases 'excellent' by HMI in a 1992 inspection.

The development of the Business Education PGCE introduced the notion of 'days in partnership schools', building upon inputs provided at the university. The possibility of students spending three days a week in schools was considered at this time but ruled out by the planning team of teachers and university lecturers who felt that this placed too great a demand upon schools (interestingly, this transpired a year later anyway, with the advent of the professional year, described below). Eventually, it was determined that students would spend two days in school and three days in the university and schools were provided with guidelines as to those areas which it was considered appropriate for them to develop with the students on placement.

These new initiatives resulted in a variety of partnerships. In some schools, teaching practice followed the traditional model, with assessment being undertaken by university tutors, in others, supervision and assessment were largely the responsibility of trained schoolteacher mentors. Although it would have been preferable to operate with one partnership model, it was clear that any true notion of partnership would need to reflect the needs and wishes of all parties. It was recognised, however, that the traditional model of university support would eventually have to be phased out in accordance with the requirements of Circular 9/92.

The increase in the number of business education students, together with the decline in the subject's importance in the school syllabus, led to a potential shortage of school placements and subsequent employment opportunities. Students often tend to seek employment in the geographical area in which they have trained, and there was concern that the significant number of business education students graduating from the university was leading to a shortage of available teaching positions. For these reasons, existing links with boroughs and counties in the south east of England were strengthened and opportunities for placements sought. In 1991, Sunderland students were placed in schools in the London Borough of Havering, an arrangement that has been maintained. These placements have been supervised in the traditional manner with assessment largely remaining the university tutor's responsibility. With the advent of Circular 9/92 and the need for closer partnerships, university tutors have worked with LEA advisers and teachers in Kent and Havering on training programmes for school based tutors in order that they might eventually take the major responsibility for student placements. While the main focus of the training has been on how school and college tutors will supervise, advise and assess students on placement, feedback from the students who undertook placements in the south-east in the early years demonstrated that the students needed wider support mechanisms. These included carefully thought out lodging arrangements, access to an educational resource centre and placements which enabled Sunderland students to meet together to give mutual support. Certainly the work undertaken with Havering and Kent has been invaluable in the development of our partnership schemes and this year Havering is accommodating ten final year students for teaching practice. In Kent the partnership is developing on two fronts, some schools are now entering a more integral phase of partnership as school based tutors, while others continue to use an LEA adviser as the student's supervisor.

In the autumn of 1992, it was resolved that the School of Education should enter the university's modular Credit Accumulation and Transfer scheme in September 1993. This meant that not only would all courses need to be reviewed and rewritten to comply with the modular scheme but also that they should incorporate the requirements of Circular 9/92. The shift to school-based teacher training resulted in a realisation that asking schools to accept students following a variety of different courses: four year and two year BEds and PGCE would not only prove immensely complex, it would also disadvantage the university in its quest for school places.

Complexity

School-based teacher training requires considerably more understanding by all members of any university and school partnership as to the nature and timing of the various course inputs. Topics covered within the university need to be explored and considered in specific school contexts and opportunities provided for students to discuss their ideas and opinions with school-based tutors in the light of their experiences. For this reason, it is essential that these tutors have a clear understanding of the week by week programme. This becomes problematic when students arrive with very different backgrounds. Consider, for example, a school that is receiving students from a university offering a range of courses of varying length and design with undergraduates and postgraduates. Student 'A' could be in the third year of a four-year technology with education course; student

'B' in the second year of a two-year maths with education degree while student 'C; might be pursuing a PGCE in modern foreign languages. To have a different school-based structure for each of these courses could cause administrative chaos. In addition to the variety of topics under consideration, it would be difficult for school-based tutors to identify the differing stages of professional development reached by students pursuing different courses and plan suitable experiences accordingly.

The need for school places

The architects of the university's school-based scheme recognised that current pressures experienced by many schools could result in at least an initial reluctance to enter into partnerships for school-based training. In a situation in which there might be a scarcity of school places and doubts as to the demands which the new model might make upon already overstretched school staff, it was considered essential to offer a programme that would prove both attractive and easily understood. It was considered that the complex nature of the University of Sunderland's degrees might prove unattractive to schools who would be likely to find it easier to work solely with PGCE students. A simpler model of professional training was deemed essential.

Thus, for wholly pragmatic reasons, in particular the need to establish a manageable suite of courses that would attract schools into partnership, there evolved a recognition that a uniform one-year course of professional training was the most effective way forward. Students training as secondary school teachers would follow this course, called the professional year, whichever programme they were following—two-year BEd, four-year BEd or PGCE.

In order for such a scheme to operate it was recognised as essential that students could demonstrate appropriate subject knowledge to function as specialist subject teachers. In the case of the two-year BEd, therefore, it was clearly necessary for the year of professional training to take place in the second year. The first year of the degree, (building upon students' earlier higher education experience, such as an HND course) was to be devoted to the furtherance of subject knowledge and would be generally unrelated to academic or professional aspects of education. In order to ensure that students had sufficient subject knowledge, there were no opportunities to engage in the study of education other than during the professional year.

The four-year honours degrees in business education and technology education offered rather more opportunities for the study of education both as an academic discipline and as a professional undertaking. Professional training would be included as an integral part of a four-year programme (qualified teacher status being awarded by means of an intercalated Certificate of Education), in which academic study of education issues would be developed in the light of professional experience. For this reason, it was decided that the professional year would operate in the third year of this degree, sandwiched between two years of mainly subject knowledge and one year of education. Inputs on the nature and provision of education and on the topic of teaching and learning would, however, be provided in years one and two. The varying programme structures are demonstrated in Figure 6.1.

4-year programmes	2-year programmes	PGCE
Year 1—subject study + education		
Year 2—subject study + education	Year 1—subject study	
Year 3—professional year	Year 2—professional year	professional year
Year 4—education + subject study		

Figure 6.1   BEd/PGCE course structures incorporating a common year of professional training

The fourth year of the degree involves study of a wide range of education modules including:

- specialist subject teaching in school and college settings

- generic options examining such issues as adolescent development, special educational needs, personal and social education, educational assessment

- an opportunity to travel overseas in order to undertake a comparative analysis of educational practice.

The great advantage of a common professional year is that partners in schools can assume that all students placed with them start from a similar position, that is, from one of professional naivety. Of course, in practice a number of within-course and between-course differences are always likely to exist. Unlike students on the one- and two-year courses, four-year BEd students will already have studied some education modules and will not come 'cold' to the professional year. There are also likely to be differences in subject knowledge, for example, PGCE students, although graduates in an appropriate discipline, might find it more difficult than their colleagues on BEd courses to demonstrate certain knowledge-based aspects required by the National Curriculum. This is particularly likely to be the case in technology where students' initial degrees do not always map easily onto National Curriculum topics.

Learning to become a teacher can often lead students to feel inadequate and deskilled. A consequence of this may be a sudden and incautious decision that teaching is not to be one's future profession. Historically, the role of the tutor in schools of education incorporated an important supportive, empowering function which reflected an understanding that student teachers needed opportunities to gain an adequate perspective and understanding both of the nature of teaching and of themselves as developing professionals. The competing pressures on teachers' time, in which the resolution of student anxiety may sometimes be perceived as a lesser imperative, may preclude opportunities for the sometimes lengthy periods of counselling and guidance which are necessary for those students who experience role confusion or self-doubt. In addition, many teachers express concern that they lack the necessary skills to help students who are confused about professional and personal aspects of their lives. In many schools, student teachers are still perceived as 'belonging to' the university, and ultimate responsibility for student welfare perceived as resting with the university tutor.

In some situations, the much reduced availability and accessibility of university tutors may leave students feeling somewhat 'stateless', not really part of the school and, during the phase of professional training, not really part of the university. A key issue for BEd course teams concerns the extent to which relationships with university staff, developed during the initial part of the two- and four-year BEd degrees, can be maintained during a professional year that sees students spending the majority of their time in school.

The professional year

The main purpose of this part of the BEd degree programme is to provide a course of professional training that will enable students to develop those skills that will ensure that they become efficient and purposeful teachers For this reason, it is primarily concerned with the practical issues of day-to-day teaching in classroom, workshop and laboratory. The content is guided by DFE Circular 9/92 and central to it are those competencies that are outlined as appropriate for beginning teachers.

The structure of the year is outlined in Figure 6.2. As students are required to spend 120 days in school, and, for various reasons (e.g. holidays, illnesses) gaps are likely to occur, the programme has built in opportunities for 130 days, ten days extra.

Key aspects of the programme are modules one and two. Here,

Week No.	1993/4 Week Beg.		Days in School
-1	13/9/93	**Participant Observation in School (Primary)**	10
0	20/9/93		
TERM 1			
1	27/9/93	**Induction and Professional Orientation**	
2	4/10/03		
3	11/10/93	**Module 1**	
4	18/10/93	**University** **Linked School Experience**	15
5	25/10/93	**2 days** **3 days**	
6	1/11/93		
7	8/11/93	**School Experience (paired)** (equivalent of one day per week for reflection and evaluation)	
8	15/11/93		
9	22/11/93		25
10	29/11/93		
11	6/12/93		
12	13/12/93	**Review**	
TERM 2			
1	10/1/94	**Module 2**	
2	17/1/94		
3	24/1/94	**University** **Linked School Experience**	15
4	31/1/95	**2 days** **3 days**	
5	7/2/94		
6	14/2/94		
7	21/2/94		
8	28/2/94	**School Experience** (equivalent of one day per week for reflection and evaluation)	
9	7/3/94		35
10	14/3/94		
11	21/3/94		
12	28/3/94		
TERM 3			
1	11/4/94	**School experience** (continued)	
2	18/4/94		20
3	25/4/94		
4	2/5/94		
5	9/5/94	**Review**	
6	16/5/94		
7	23/5/94	**Module 3**	
8	30/5/94	**Option modules**	
9	6/6/94	(including a minimum of ten days school based activity)	10
10	13/6/94		
11	20/6/94	**Two half modules or one full module.**	Total 130

Same local school }

Figure 6.2   The structure of the professional year

students attend the university on Mondays and Fridays and are based in their host school for the remaining three days. The topics for exploration, which largely reflect the 9/92 competencies, are agreed by school and university staff in advance; an arrangement that provides a valuable opportunity for students to relate their work in the university to a specific school context.

One topic, for example, concerns the management of behaviour in school, a feature of initial teacher education that has been highlighted as essential by the present Government. For this topic, students, in the university are provided with a conceptual framework with which to consider those factors that lead to the maintenance of discipline. Through the use of lectures and seminars, simulations and video they are helped to recognise how they may convey a sense of authority to children, prevent and manage misbehaviour and appreciate the value, or otherwise, of punishment and rewards. In school, they explore with teachers the formal aspects of maximising positive behaviour (e.g. the school's policy on discipline, sanctions employed, the way by which school rules operate) and the more informal, interpersonal aspects (e.g. the nature of teacher-pupil relationships, the expectations of, and degrees of tolerance for children's behaviour). Finally, the students are asked to examine their own functioning by considering their non-verbal behaviour (rate, volume and pitch of their voice, their use of posture, gestures, space, touch and territory) and their oral behaviour (in particular, how they use language as a means of social control). The opportunity to develop such professional skills based on decontextualised theoretical/conceptual frameworks which are subsequently explored by means of simulations, dialogue with experienced teachers and self-examination within a specific classroom situation, perhaps provides students with ideal circumstances to learn transferable and generalisable skills appropriate for a variety of school contexts.

It has been noted (Miles et al. 1993) that the number of days students spend in school is not necessarily a valuable indicator of the extent of teacher involvement in their training. The need to respond quickly to Circular 9/92 was hindered by the need to develop modularised programmes and the need to explore fully whether a school-based model could operate over a two- or four-year period. This reduced opportunities for prolonged and detailed consultation with a wide range of potential school partners and initial dialogue tended to operate with those schools where the closest relationships had already been established. A much wider range of schools and individual teachers was canvassed about the professional year once a proposed architecture was established, and the draft scheme was fully circulated in the hope that any structural and procedural flaws could be identified and remedied prior to its first year of operation.

Where schools expressed concern about the proposed scheme, issues tended to focus on the viability and difficulties of any school-based ITT model rather than with the specifics of our proposed scheme.

It was recognised that real partnership was more likely to occur once the course architecture and procedures were established and teachers were able to reflect on its operation. This has proved to be the case and after an initial stage, when most teachers were endeavouring to grasp the mechanics of a school-based model and the significant change in their role (by no means fully understood from the outset, however voluminous and detailed the paperwork) the willingness of many teachers to adopt a proactive role in the evolution of the programme is snowballing. The partnership between university and school staff is now realised through many avenues:

- Teachers and university staff collaborate in the development of student learning materials. The need for high quality supported self-study material is recognised yet its production will necessarily be a long and time-consuming process. The complemetary skills and perspectives of teacher colleagues have greatly assisted us in our attempts to develop meaningful, relevant and challenging materials and activities.

- Collaboration in recruitment and admissions procedures.

- The establishment of school clusters (3–6 schools) where materials and procedures are developed and discussed.

- Reflection, discussion, and negotiation about current developments at moderation and planning sessions attended by all partnership schools.

- Teacher membership of various university programme and module studies' boards and validation panels.

It was recognised that the flow of information between schools and university was potentially problematic. School-based training was likely to increase significantly the degree of contact between institutions and it was recognised that schools would need to be linked with a key figure in the university who would act as the first point of contact as issues and difficulties arose. Each school was, therefore, allocated a member of university staff (termed a school liaison tutor) whose responsibilities were to:

- become a regular point of contact
- deal with all initial queries
- to provide help, guidance and advice on professional year matters

- ● ensure that standards of the teaching of professional year students are maintained
- ● ensure that standards of assessment of teaching competencies are maintained.

School liaison tutors are required to visit each school on a fortnightly basis to discuss the operation of the professional year. Usually, the point of contact was that member of the school's staff who had responsibility for overseeing the programme although meetings are also arranged with students and teachers in their appropriate subject departments.

It was agreed that all visits to schools by any member of university academic or research staff needed to be arranged in consultation with the appropriate school liaison tutor in order to ensure that unnecessary and/or excessive visits did not take place. The difficulties of alienating university colleagues, who might not appreciate any perceived constraints upon access to schools, was recognised yet, in practice, the need to ensure that schools did not feel overburdened was widely accepted.

It is, of course, essential that university and school subject specialists also have an opportunity to meet and discuss the students' progress. During each placement, therefore, students are jointly observed by subject specialists. Shared observation sessions not only ensure that the work in school and in the university is coherent and integrated, it also helps to ensure that standards and expectations are consistent across schools.

The role of the school liaison tutor has proven particularly important to the operation of our partnership. Most schools have greatly valued the regular support and guidance of a university tutor who, in many cases, has become a friend of the school, sometimes attending school functions such as concerts and prize-giving. This function, however, makes significant demands upon university staff time and one must question whether future funding will permit such a role to be maintained.

The competent teacher

DFE Circular 9/92's identification of specific professional competencies required of students in order for them to gain Qualified Teacher Status may have significant implications for the model of the teacher held by all those involved in initial teacher education. Although other university and college schools of education have chosen to rewrite the competencies or embed them in alternative means of assessment, the professional year has adopted a profiling scheme in which the 9/92 competencies are validated within a Record of Achievement model. Consistent with this model, students are required to provide evidence (e.g. from teaching practice files, tutor feedback) to school and university staff to support their claims to competency.

The university provides a profile report form for each of the DFE competencies and schools are welcome to add to these if they wish. Each form provides space for:

- the student to give his/her account of progress and difficulties

- references to evidence of achievement of competences

- the tutors' (university and school) views of progress

- signatures indicating validation of the evidence of achievement

- specific targets for action to improve future performance.

The procedure is designed to encourage regular target setting, assessment, record keeping and progress reviews. By placing the onus for collecting evidence upon the students, it endeavours to encourage them to be proactive in their work with schools and assume responsibility for demonstrating and articulating their developing skills and knowledge.

This procedure can place enormous strains upon a partnership. Schools have differed in the extent to which they have placed responsibility for providing evidence of competency in the hands of students. As a result, student experience of the assessment process has varied. Perhaps a more fundamental difficulty, however, concerns the need to establish a shared understanding on the part of all those involved in the assessment process as to what represents the achievement of a competency. Specific difficulties relate to issues of timing, interpretation and standardisation, progression and teachers' conceptions of what constitutes professional competency. Each of these is briefly discussed below.

Timing

Although the University of Sunderland suggests that the achievement of competencies should take place in 'drip-feed' manner throughout students' placement in school, many school-based tutors have preferred to wait until the last week of the placement before undertaking the validation procedure. It is argued, quite reasonably, that it is at this time that the student's ability as a teacher can be best gauged. Furthermore, consideration of competencies at one meeting may be significantly less time-consuming. For some students, however, this apparent delay in validation can cause heightened levels of anxiety and doubt, especially if this process is delayed by unforeseen absence through illness.

Discussion between the partners in group sessions indicates that school-based tutors vary greatly on this issue and, in this case, it may prove necessary to recognise that schools will not act uniformly in this respect.

Interpretation and standardisation

When the National Curriculum was implemented, teachers frequently objected to the fact that Statements of Attainment, the instruments of criterion referenced assessment, were open to diverse interpretation and suggested a wholly spurious form of standardisation (Elliott 1990; Waterson 1994). Gradually, by means of ongoing moderation and standardisation, a greater degree of shared understanding has been achieved. The introduction of listed student competencies in DFE Circular 9/92 appears to mirror the above situation. The competencies may appear relatively straightforward to the naive reader yet, as with National Curriculum, problems of interpretation and standardisation are considerable. To illustrate, consider a competency such as:

> Students should demonstrate that they can create and maintain
> a purposeful and orderly environment for the pupils

This may be widely interpreted by different individuals not only between but also within institutions. Does the competency require students to be able to manage classes that are problematic for experienced and capable teachers? Should one take into account the type of school (e.g. independent versus inner-city)? How can one reconcile the observation that a student is 'competent' on a first placement but has immense difficulties in a subsequent one?

In operating the profile, the university has been asked by school partners to offer increasingly specific guidance as to what constitutes successful achievement of a competency. Initial guidelines were supplemented by more detailed material, although it was generally recognised that, as with Statements of Attainment, this issue would only be tackled by the achievement of shared understandings gleaned over time. The regular partnership meetings, at which specific competencies are discussed, analysed and contextualised by reference to actual student performance in schools, are proving to be an effective means of establishing such a shared consensus although, as with National Curriculum, the subjectivity of the assessment process and the context-dependency of performance can never be fully overcome.

Progression

Once having obtained a competence, how can students and beginning teachers demonstrate progression in the relevant area? In the university's ITT profiling scheme there is scope for students to demonstrate competence at a higher level by entering these on the profile record forms. It is interesting to note that some schools have asked whether regression can take place, that is, whether the achievement of competency on one's first teaching practice can be cancelled out if it is not demonstrated on a subsequent placement. Although an achieved competency cannot be revoked, there may be difficulties, which will need to be resolved, if a student's motivation and subsequent performance were to reduce during the course of the year.

In considering a need for progression, a number of schools (see, for example, Sandhill View School—this chapter) recognising that professional development is an ongoing process, have built upon the profile in order to provide an induction programme for newly qualified teachers.

What is a competent teacher?

In the university's documentation the designers of the professional year state:

> inherent in (the) model is a view of the teacher as a questioning, analytical and reflective person who has the ability to apply knowledge and skills in making informed judgements and to evaluate alternative solutions to educational issues and problems in school and classroom.

To what extent, however, can the model of the reflective practitioner be reconciled with a programme in which a significant element involves the demonstration of specific competencies? Carr (1993) argues that competency-based approaches are inimical to the pursuit and attainment of the reflective practitioner, for the latter involves:

> ... the rational initiation of students into forms of discourse and modes of conduct which are by no means settled or decided (p.2).

In a national survey of Initial Teacher Education in England and Wales during 1990–91, Miles et al. (1993) clearly differentiate between those courses offering the reflective practitioner model (72 per cent) as opposed to the competency model (6 per cent). It would, perhaps, be interesting to note whether, in the light of Circular 9/92, responses by teachers and/or university tutors would now differ.

Carr contends that teacher educators are being required to forsake a model that asks students to think and respond flexibly, rationally and creatively to those educational challenges which may exist in a particular time and/or context. Instead, he considers that we have adopted a narrow, instrumental approach whose exigent imperatives reinforce a spurious consensus as to what it is to be a competent teacher. The danger that competencies may be seen as discrete, compartmentalised elements, which fail to be integrated in practice was a recurrent concern voiced during a series of NCC/CATE/SEAC conferences held in the first quarter of 1993 (NCC 1993). In addition, there are very real dangers that some students are seeing the gaining of competencies as an activity only tangentially related to the business of functioning in the classroom.

A further difficulty is that some teachers may prefer to make a more global judgement of the student based upon rather more impressionistic evidence. Having made a decision about the student's ability and suitability, possibly largely based on a range of interpersonal and motivational factors, the teacher may consider discrete competencies to be an intrusive irrelevance that can be 'signed off' almost in blanket fashion.

As one means of quality control, the university requires all professional year students to submit their profile record forms, together with teacher signatory validation, to a member of the university staff. In a brief interview, the student and tutor discuss the evidence supplied for each competency. The potential for tension within the partnership could be significant if the university tutor were to consider that global judgements by school tutors had replaced, or were not supported by, consideration of the competencies or, alternatively, whether there was disagreement between the partners as to whether a specific competency had been demonstrated. Happily, perhaps as a result of the close liaison between the university and schools, this difficulty has yet to surface. Potentially difficult situations are discussed by the respective school-based tutor and university liaison tutor with the latter then briefing the university tutor responsible for competency validation.

Working in partnership—Sandhill View School

Sandhill View school is an 11–16 mixed comprehensive school, set in parkland between two large council estates on the south west side of the City of Sunderland. Both estates were built shortly after the second world war. The catchment area also includes part of a large pre-war council estate and a very small private estate to the west. Within the catchment area, there are high levels of unemployment, single parent families and significant socio-economic disadvantage.

The present building was erected as a 'show school' and opened in 1953 as two secondary modern schools, 1974 saw the introduction of comprehensive education with a roll of 1996 pupils. By 1981 this roll had fallen to 850 and by 1986 to 332.

In 1987 Sandhill View was born of the amalgamation with a neighbourhood comprehensive as part of a local authority reorganisation programme. The school was designated as 6FE and has grown in size from about 450 pupils to the present 800.

Prior to amalgamation the two schools offered their services to a number of teacher training establishments. Students were generally required to participate in a six or ten week block practice with an observation period prior to each practice. Assessment was primarily the responsibility of the university although there was input from the school. The main focus for each practice was that of teaching a specific subject within the classroom for about 80 per cent of the week. (Students were then given the opportunity to attend residential courses when the timing coincided with practice dates.)

With the advent of school-based training, Sandhill View looked to build on what was essentially a skeleton approach to training teachers within a school. We made a decision very early on to work with one teacher training establishment in order to ease administration and enable us to forge closer working partnerships with our university colleagues. Our long term objectives could only be met if we employed this strategy. It was also extremely important that all communications were made through a 'key person', when liaising with a large institution such as the University of Sunderland. Chaos, in terms of timetabling, staff supervision, and overuse of specific classes would soon rule if communications were not handled effectively.

Perhaps one of the weaknesses of many secondary school teaching practices is that students have tended to be located within a particular subject area and have not always been enabled to grasp the true breadth and diversity of the teacher's role. It may be that this phenomenon explains, or at least reinforces, the reluctance of some teachers to become involved with such issues as personal, health, moral and social education. The statement, 'I'm a teacher of mathematics, not . . .' may reflect a rather narrow conception of one's role as a teacher which, in part, results from a rather narrow focus of training.

Students have also been given the opportunity of supporting our school activities and enterprise week. About twenty students are involved on an annual basis. Activities are varied and have included outdoor education, mini-enterprise, forest sculpture, building a wildlife sanctuary, to mention a few. The approach to this week is less formal than in most classroom situations and students have tended to find the opportunity to consider alternative ways of working with children most informative, with student involvement providing reciprocal benefits to the school.

From 1989, students were offered the opportunity to work with our special needs teachers for one half day each week. This was purely voluntary and done in each student's own time. The benefit to the school in terms of extra bodies in these specialist areas is enormous and had undoubtedly contributed to recent successes with slow learners.

By 1992, the number of visits in connection with students had increased significantly. Students were visiting the school to obtain information for course work assignments, team teaching outside block practices, or coming along for vocational awareness-raising sessions prior to applying for a university place. The modern foreign language department agreed to pilot a new programme of 'teacher mentorship' which shifted the emphasis from university to school-based assessment during teaching practice. There proved to be some teething troubles with regard to communication as the 'key person' was not always informed about various activities. This was largely because a direct line existed between university tutors and those class teachers who were involved in the scheme. For this reason, the more structured lines of communication established by the present school-based model (see above) have been greatly welcomed.

In September 1993, Sandhill View entered into a full partnership contract with the University of Sunderland involving mathematics, modern languages, music, science and technology departments. This scheme, the professional year, outlined above, reflects the shift towards school-based teacher training. There are financial, as well as professional rewards although it is recognised that the available resources are such that school-based teacher training is unlikely to become a significant means of generating income. Sandhill View's motivation for entering into the partnership is not merely the result of a recognition that a future generation of teachers needs to be trained, it is also because responsibility for training students has become an important means of professional development for our own staff. The process of assisting others to develop professionally has resulted in many of our colleagues reconsidering and re-examining their own practice. In addition, our developing induction programme for newly qualified teachers interfaces with the professional year in as seamless a fashion as possible and in line with the continuous nature of teachers' professional development as articulated in Circular 9/92.

School-based teacher training has necessitated more detailed examination of teachers' specific roles. In accordance with the university's suggestion we have differentiated between generic tutors who have an overview of, and responsibility for, the whole school experience, and subject tutors whose primary concern is subject specific teaching within the classroom. The generic tutor, known in Sandhill View as the 'professional tutor' has major responsibility for the assessment of student competencies. The school has four professional tutors, comprising myself (who also acts as the 'key person' with overall responsibility for school-based training) and three senior teachers whose background, personality and experience make them ideally suited for this role.

The introduction of the new school-based programme has enabled Sandhill View to work with the university on providing a much greater variety of experiences for students. Prior to the commencement of this new programme, university staff spent a training day in school with senior staff during which time consideration was given to those student experiences which were essential or desirable and how and when these might be introduced. These included, visits to feeder primary schools, meetings with the educational psychologist, careers officer and educational welfare officer, parents' evenings and community events. Work shadowing is seen as a valuable ingredient, enabling the observer a greater perception and understanding of school life and opportunities are provided for students to shadow both staff and school students.

Naturally these are early days and there have and will continue to be difficulties. The majority of these will be gradually overcome as the partnership grows and strengthens. Despite the extensive paperwork and regular meetings, it is only through the operation of the programme that the respective roles of school and university staff in supervision, assessment and counselling will be fully understood by all parties. Fortunately, we enjoy an excellent relationship with our local university and difficulties are explored in a positive and constructive climate.

Partnership implies far more than merely accepting students on placement. Sandhill View teachers are now involved in developing the professional year by their membership on various University Boards of Study, by leading training sessions for potential and existing school-based tutors, and by assisting in the writing of associated professional and academic materials.

Evaluation and pointers to the future—the end of the Bachelor of Education degree?

As the professional training of teachers has become more centred upon the school, many university and college education departments have explored the viability of offering education as an academic discipline leading to a BA or BSc (Education). This would permit a number of permutations to operate; some students, for example, who have no intention to become teachers, might wish to study education as part of a joint honours or combined honours (n.b. combined honours programmes involve the selection of modules from a number of different academic disciplines) programme.

Those wishing to become teachers, on the other hand, might wish to follow a joint honours programme comprising education and a subject study of one of the disciplines of the National Curriculum. For this latter group, the professional training element would be the professional year awarded as a PGCE or, alternatively, as an intercalated Certificate of Education.

Many intending teachers might find the above combination an excellent preparation for the demands and pressures of professional training. For many students undergoing such training, the need to develop classroom survival skills is paramount and there is rarely sufficient opportunity for sustained reading and reflection. A joint honours degree in an academic subject such as history, together with the study of education, could equip students with a sufficient command of a National Curriculum subject and a knowledge and understanding of teaching and learning processes which could valuably underpin a school-based course of professional training.

Governmental regulations that Bachelor of Education degrees must include Qualified Teacher Status have greatly disadvantaged those students who, in their final years of study, fail to demonstrate necessary professional competence. Such students not only fail in their endeavours to become teachers, they also receive no academic award. If, however, students registered for BA/BSc degrees in education, with professional training as a discrete activity, those who proved unsuitable for teaching could still attain graduate status.

A further change in education degrees is likely to be a shortening of the length of training courses. The Government has expressed a desire to reduce four-year teacher training programmes to three years. It is difficult to see, however, how an honours degree with qualified teacher status can be achieved in this lesser timespan. One possibility is that a significant number of students might prefer to enrol on a three-year pass degree in education involving two years of academic study and one year of professional training. Such a degree is likely to appeal particularly to mature students with family commitments (a high proportion of those studying at the University of Sunderland) for whom four years of university study is often a financial struggle.

The University of Sunderland already operates a part-time in-service programme for practising teachers who wish to convert their pass degree in education to one at honours level. An honours component to a professional degree, such as education, presupposes a body of experience. Shifting the honours component of the award to an in-service, post-experience workplace setting, meets Government requirements and may prove more professionally appropriate.

A major difficulty arising from the new university–school partnerships concerns assessment. Although few universities would dispute the suggestion that schools are well-equipped to make judgements as to the suitability of students for qualified teacher status, difficulties arise when teaching practice grades are used in the classification of degrees. Whereas the traditional BEd degrees tended to involve university and school tutors in, at times prolonged, discussion and negotiation, the new model leaves major decisions to the school. The difficulties of ensuring equity of assessment within and between schools and the limited roles of university staff in standardisation and moderation have resulted in a widespread recognition that the assessment of professional practice may be best kept as a discrete activity unrelated to degree classification.

The nature of future partnerships is difficult to forecast. Teacher training in England and Wales, by reducing the focus upon the academic study of education, has moved away from most European models at a time when the prevailing trend of 'Europeanisation' is likely to require greater harmonisation of training programmes. It is difficult to predict, at the present time, whether any shift towards common routes of education and training will lead the teacher training pendulum to swing back towards a more traditional model.

New three-year degrees and school-based models of training may not permit the new teacher to analyse and reflect upon, to a sufficient extent such issues as, the academic content of the National Curriculum appropriate teaching and learning strategies, and those basic research skills which all teachers require to evaluate the quality of their performance. Student teachers may find that they have opportunities to gain little more than a passing acquaintance with the skills, knowledge and understanding which are core components of the teacher as a professional. Schools are the most appropriate settings to practise and contextualise yet they may not provide the space and time for study and reflection. Whether any shortfall in the existing balance of activity will be reconciled by further changes of partnership roles or by reallocating the proportion of time spent in school is currently unclear.

Consideration of the future of teacher training should not merely focus upon the structure, length and setting of courses. Equally, it should address the potential shifts of role for school and university staff.

For a variety of reasons, not all schoolteachers believe that training student teachers is an appropriate function for them to under-take. Where this view is held by a minority of staff, some schools may respond by involving only those colleagues who are committed to the scheme. Greater difficulty may exist in those circumstances where a willingness to undertake the tutor's role extends only to a narrow emphasis upon specific aspects of classroom practice. Such a perspective may result in students adopting relatively mechanistic and instrumental approaches which are unlikely to assist them to grasp the complex and problematic nature of teaching and learning.

A narrow conception of the tutor role may lead to an inability to reconcile any potential conflict between the needs of the student and those of the school. This may not merely concern resource issues, such as the amount of time which can be devoted to student support, but also the strained relationship which can arise from a perceived challenge to, or criticism of, a school's philosophy or culture. Although the greater contextualisation provided by school-based training can be of great value to students, there is a danger that, in some instances, students may feel that their own needs are marginal to those of the school. In her study of the operation of one PGCE course, Williams (1993) noted that:

> ... a common criticism of the advice offered within the school
> is that it reflects an individual school culture or policy
> excessively and takes insufficient account of the possibility of
> alternative strategies which might be more effective for an
> individual student. This, of course, raises important questions
> about the extent to which conflict can occur between the needs
> of the school and the needs of the student and how such conflict
> can be minimised (p.410).

Most school-based tutors will recognise that the primary role of the school is to educate children. Many school-based tutors will need not only to find an acceptable balance between this function and the, sometimes competing task of training teachers, but also to recognise the importance of both contextualised and decontextualised experiences.

The burgeoning literature on teachers' perceptions of, and adjustment to, their new roles in school-based training has in no way been matched by a parallel examination of university tutors. Many university personnel have found it difficult to come to terms with the diminution of their role, particularly given the ongoing assault upon their professional and theoretical knowledge base (Lunt et al. 1993), and the potential threats to their future livelihood. Some have found it paradoxical that they have been required to canvass schools to take over an aspect of work which they do not want to relinquish. In such circumstances, it will be necessary for both university and school staff to recognise that partnerships will only prove effective where there exists mutual respect, trust and goodwill.

Earlier in this chapter it was noted that many schools consider students 'to belong to the university' and, therefore, it is university staff who should intervene when students require counselling on personal matters or support in professional aspects only tangentially related to teaching. University tutors may also be happy to see this position maintained, yet financial constraints are likely to place a limit upon the amount of ongoing support which they can provide to students on placement. It has already been noted that this dilemma may be at its greatest when school-based professional training is sandwiched between two or more years of academic study. If current models of school-based teacher training are to be maintained, however, the more holistic view of students' needs, together with a high degree of teacher support, evidenced in a number of schools, may need to become widely accepted by all parties.

In summary, Bachelor of Education degrees for secondary teachers are, perhaps, a thing of the past. In their place we are likely to see BA and BSc degrees in education with both academic and professional elements. Those education students who intended to practise as teachers are likely to undertake a professional training course largely based in school. Assessment for qualified teacher status will be primarily undertaken by teachers (although university staff may have a moderation or standardisation function) and this will generally be unrelated to degree classification.

The respective roles and functions of school and university staff will continue to evolve. Transitional funding, provided by central government to assist the shift of school-based training, has enabled some universities and colleges to provide more intensive training and support to schools and students than is likely to be the case in the future. Financial constraints, however, are likely to continue to reduce the scope for university tutor involvement during students' time in school. All parties involved in the partnership will need to recognise that current models of school-based training place a major responsibility on school tutors to ensure that students on placement receive a high level of professional and personal support. In some cases, neither university nor school staff may find this an agreeable scenario, yet their ready acceptance of this fact will be essential if programmes are to operate effectively in the future.

Part 3
Issues for the future

7 Teacher competences and their assessment

Myra McCulloch

Introduction

In the current political context, teacher education is under attack. Its main critics are from the right wing of the Conservative Party, members of the Centre for Policy Studies, who identify irrelevant and 'subversive' theory (Lawlor 1990) as undermining the quality and effectiveness of teacher training offered in higher education institutions. In response to these criticisms and fitting nicely with the government's commitment to a more school-based approach to initial teacher training (DFE 1992) is the focus on a competence-based approach. The vocational flavour fits nicely with the emphasis on 'training' rather than education and, it could be argued, represents a political compromise for teacher educators who wish to defend, against the most radical critics, a place for higher education to make at least some contribution to training pre-service teachers. It may also represent an opportunity to show that the teaching and learning taking place in higher education reflect purposeful, systematic means by which student teachers acquire the relevant knowledge and skills to equip them to develop in their role as teachers.

The commitment to competence, however, is not at all straightforward. In the first place how is it defined? And, when defined, and central to this chapter, how is it to be assessed? There appears to be a problem emerging that a definition of competence which will permit ready assessment will not permit the continuing commitment of teacher educators to the values of a liberal education (Carr 1993). This is being challenged by those who argue that the true definition of competence implies the kind of understanding and values which underpin a liberal higher education and that these higher order characteristics can, indeed, be specified, defined, observed and assessed.

This chapter seeks to explore competing definitions of competence and to relate these to issues of assessment, particularly in relation to initial teacher education.

Definitions of competence

Recent statements on the reform of secondary teacher training make explicit the need 'to focus more clearly on the results of training' (DES 1992a). Circular 9/92 (DFE 1992) recognises that statements of competences expected of newly qualified teachers 'do not purport to provide a complete syllabus for initial teacher training' (para 11) but in Annex 2 Para 2.1 the following statement can be found 'Higher Education Institutions, schools and students should focus on the competences of teaching throughout the whole period of initial training. The progressive development of these competences should be monitored regularly during initial training. Their attainment at a level appropriate to newly qualified teachers should be the objective of every student taking a course of initial training' (para 2.1). What does not appear in these government documents is any fundamental discussion of what competence means and how it can be assessed, though the equivalent papers in Scotland do seek to define their terms. '... professional competences, the word should be taken to refer to knowledge, understanding and attitudes, as well as to practical skills. In order to teach satisfactorily, certain craft skills have undoubtedly to be mastered. But in addition teachers must have a knowledge and understanding ... content ... process ... and must be able to evaluate and justify their procedures' (The Scottish Office Education Department 1992). Carr (1993) argues, however, that this 'is presumably meant to disarm or forestall the criticism that competence approaches are crudely reductionist' (p.18). Indeed, the major criticism of the competence movement is that its behaviourist foundation assumes understanding from observed behaviour whereas the link between the two is more problematic.

The lack of consensual specificity of meaning and the omission of any apparent concern with how assessment schemes might relate to such new style courses reflects the current state of the debate. What are the competing definitions of competence? And how might they be operationalised and assessed?

Wood and Power (1987) suggest that competence is used in two different ways. Firstly, in an atheoretical way to signify enhanced performance and secondly by theorising about competence as the deep structure responsible for the surface performance. If we study competence, we are considering a working model of the development of expertise; studying performance, on the other hand raises methodological problems about how what a person can do relates to what s/he really understands. In other words, competence is what a person knows and can do under ideal circumstances while performance is what is actually done under existing circumstances. Competence embraces the structure of knowledge and abilities whilst performance includes also the processes of 'accessing and utilising those structures and a host of affective, motivational, attentional and stylistic factors that influence the ultimate response' (Messick 1984).

Problems of assessment

In order to achieve successful task performance, students must possess the structure embodied in the task (competence) and the operating rules which permit them to process the information from a task and produce a result or performance. This raises two questions for assessors; first how to cope with the fact that in order to achieve successful task performance, triggers might be needed—prompts, hints, clarifications—so that the deep, structural competence can be accessed. Wood and Power (1987) discuss this in terms of Vygotsky's zone of proximal development i.e. the gap between the present level of development and the potential level based on what the students can do as long as they have help. This implies an assessment mode which seeks to measure the strengths of students— what they can do in the best possible circumstances, rather than their weaknesses—what they can do without contextual clarification, alternative task definitions and so on. The second problem is how to derive from performance (classroom behaviour), statements about unobservable competence (understanding). In observing performance, inconsistencies always arise, both in the observation and in the performance itself. In developmental terms, it may be argued that the tasks set to elicit competence or the methods used in presenting tasks and scoring answers don't go together. In real life people are often applying themselves to tasks and situations which they only partly understand. In order to assess competence, therefore, we may want to describe a set of contexts (range statements) within which a performance may be observed before we are willing to attribute performance to competence. We may also wish to engage in training (even while assessing) in order to gain the best possible performance—and also to transform the testing situation to an explicit learning experience. There is a danger that training may produce performance without competence but the range statements should attend to this difficulty. The assessment of students on school experience offers interesting possibilities for this mode of assessment, particularly in relation to developments of mentorship schemes involving teachers, tutors and students in a collaborative framework.

In defining competence, Wood and Power (1987) offer two versions: either 'The ability to use knowledge, product and process skills, and, as a result, act effectively to achieve a purpose' or 'The possession and development of sufficient skills, knowledge, appropriate attitudes and experience for successful performance in life roles' (p.414). In both cases there is an implication that competence is the product of education, training or other experience, distinguishable from 'competencies' by its reliance on the ability to structure and restructure knowledge, adapt to circumstances and coordinate appropriate abilities and knowledge (Messick 1984). Successful conceptualisation of competence would show how specific competencies are integrated at a higher level. Wood and Power (1987) cite studies of 'novice' and 'expert' practitioners which permit assessment of the significant differences in the knowledge bases brought to bear on problem solving at the extreme ends of the competent/incompetent continuum.

Indeed, one might wish to distinguish between threshold or continuous competences; comprehensive approaches to competence where all performers might be expected to succeed as compared with those competences achieved only by superior performers or between discrete and integrated competences (Esp 1993). In the context of classroom performance this could lead to an approach which sought to distinguish between threshold (ITE), developing professional (induction) and expert competences such as is proposed in the Review of Initial Teacher Training in Northern Ireland (DENI 1993). This scheme also sought to establish the contribution to particular learning which might be made by each of the school/HEI partners.

However, the pragmatic operational definition of competence is the level of performance obtained under elaborative procedures beyond the performance level obtained under standard conditions. And the problem with common patterns of assessment is that the standard rather than the enhanced performance is that which is measured. Wood and Power (1987) argue that resources would therefore be better invested in training teachers for assessment than in developing better tests—however good the instrument, it is dependent upon the skills of the assessor. Though they recognise that some frustration will be felt at 'spotty' inconsistent performance (Wood and Power p.420) for the responses students give 'are just as disarticulated, reflecting, or so it appears, haphazard learning ex-

periences which have not, as yet, and may never be related and co-
ordinated in order to acquire the higher-order cognitive operations
and structures which are the cornerstones of competence' (p.420).
For their definition of 'expert' implies being able to cope in all
contexts/variations/facet combinations whilst being a 'novice' means
being unable to cope with most variations; there is no transfer of
skill.

In relation to assessment this suggests that 'The purpose of
measurement, always, then, is to acquire information about attributes of objects, organisms or events' (Jones 1971). That is, 'not an
object but a property or attribute of an object'. And these attributes
must be measurable. 'To be measurable an attribute must fit the
specifications of a quantitative variable' (p.336). The implication for
teacher education is the need to identify and describe in measurable
ways the knowledge and skills which permit competencies to be
observed through performance in ways which permit the higher
order competence to be deduced. This would appear to be more
straightforward for the school based elements of initial teacher training courses.

But, it makes the assumption that a minimal acceptable level of
performance in such tasks can be specified. Glass (1978) questions
whether this can be done other than arbitrarily. He argues that the
underlying concept of achievement measurement is that there is a
continuum from no proficiency to perfect performance. At some
point along this continuum an achievement level is identified, indicated by behaviours displayed during testing, which is deemed to be
competent. Statements can therefore be made about what a student
can and cannot do, independent of reference to the performance of
others, but at a relatively arbitrary point 'pass' is awarded. This also
raises questions about the continuing competence of student
teachers and of the relevance of that 'pass' to the future demands to
be made of classroom teachers as compared with their current role.
Glass argues that whatever method of criterion determination is used
(he lists performance of others, counting backwards from 100 per
cent, bootstrapping on other criterion scores, judging minimal competence, decision-theoretic approaches and operations research) the
logic of the concept of minimal competence must be questioned. All
measures introduce an element of arbitrariness and although an
apparent clarity and objective definition is achieved, this obscures a
very complex and unclear situation. Glass suggests, therefore, that
instead of attempting to measure absolute standards we focus on
judgement about improvement and decline. In education there are
virtually no absolute standards so the assembly of comparative evidence is required—comparative experiments, norm referenced tests
and longitudinal assessments, for example. There remains the prob-

lem of how much change is enough, but, Glass argues, this is less
problematic than the problems with absolutes. Others would dispute
this view.

Messick (1984) similarly stresses the complexity of assessment in
education and makes the distinction between competence and educational achievement. Because what we are assessing represents the
structuring and restructuring of knowledge and cognitive skills, we
have to construct our assessment in developmental terms. It must
also be applied relative to intrapersonal and situational contexts
because student characteristics reflect performance; context dependent task performance is what needs to be assessed. The distinction
between competence and educational achievement reflects what an
individual can do based upon the contribution of direct instruction.
This is an important point in relation to the politics of teacher
education. If it can be argued that competence may be gained and
assessed independently from any programme of study then the relationship between courses of education and classroom teaching
becomes more difficult to defend—particularly if competence is
defined as meaning a selection of competencies evidenced in performance.

Messick (1984) emphasises understanding; the organisation of
relationships among concepts; complex systems of multiple relationships as well as organising frameworks for interpretation and action.
Educational achievement is not represented only by 'bottom up'
processing of incoming information but also by 'top down' concep-
tually driven assimilation to mental schemas or relational structures
(p.218). What is needed, therefore is a series of assessment devices
for monitoring the functional characteristics of new knowledge and
skill; for ascertaining critical differences between successful and
unsuccessful performances; for appraising the knowledge and ability
processes and structures that reveal competence in the field. Messick
argues that three characteristics should be displayed by these assessment devices—they should be diagnostic as well as judgemental;
they should permit students to demonstrate their full capacity and
they should reflect what we know about the differences between
novices and experts. Furthermore the assessor has an ethical responsibility to recognise contextual factors or contaminants and an
interpretative responsibility in making judgements about how to
take these into account.

Assessing competence in teacher education

Experience in initial teacher education so far does not display the
level of sophistication implied by Wood and Power (1987) or
Messick (1984) or, for example, studies of competences for edu-

cation management (Esp 1993). Circular 24/89 (DES 1989b) which relates to the accreditation of teacher education contained exit criteria. Circulars 9/92 (DFE 1992) and 14/93 (DFE 1993a) contain statements of competencies to be achieved through study and experience. The Council for the Accreditation of Teacher Education (CATE) relates entry criteria, course inputs and educational achievement, thus recognising a relationship between teaching and learning which is not assumed by NVQs (National Vocational Qualifications) developed in the work of the National Council for Vocational Qualifications (NCVQ) which essentially relates to the Further Education (FE) sector (CNAA 1992).

Discussions among teacher educators have employed the two types of definition discussed above: the ability to perform a task satisfactorily, the task being clearly defined and the criteria for success set out alongside, as compared with a wider definition encompassing intellectual, cognitive and attitudinal dimensions as well as performance (CNAA 1992 para 3.2 p.5). Many teacher educators, assuming only the possibilities implied by the first definition have resisted competence-based approaches because they encourage an over emphasis on skills and techniques, ignoring important aspects of teacher education, including what informs performance and arguing that the whole is more than the sum of its parts (Whitty and Willmott 1991). However, there are others within teacher education (Elliott 1989, Hextall et al. 1991) who argue that a competence-based approach can encompass the major elements within the complex and dynamic process that is teaching; evaluation, research and experimentation. These 'are not value-added features of teacher quality; they constitute the very bases of competence in teaching—that is reflectivity' (Hextall et al. 1991 p.5). 'The quality of reflectivity can be formulated as a series of competences which can be observed, developed and monitored' (p.5). The authors then go on to define some such competences. One suspects, however, that this may be a political response which attempts to fit traditional concepts of teacher education into the vocational mode currently in favour—to challenge the simplistic competency based approaches without appearing to challenge the skills based model being promoted by government.

However, although much discussion is taking place, there is little consensus about what might be identified as the competences specifically linked to the award of Qualified Teacher Status (QTS) (Whitty and Willmott 1991). Indeed there is a lack of clarity about the distinctions between and the relationships between various types of competence; some are person related; others task related; some are generic professional competences; others scores of discrete behaviours (Whitty and Willmott 1991). There is a similar lack of clarity about how performance in identified competences relates to overall 'competence'; what is needed is a concept more akin to communicative competence, derived from an underlying grammar that generates individual competences in unpredictable circumstances (Whitty and Willmott 1991).

Despite the complexity of the exercise, there are a number of advantages which can be identified in pursuing this form of teacher education. The first of these is that the definition and description of competences helps to remove the mystique from teacher education. In the current political climate this may be a somewhat poisoned chalice, but the advantage of having course objectives, readily comprehensible and clear statements of target behaviour which permit explicit evidence of progress to be gathered and allow employers to know what to expect of newly qualified teachers must be an advance on current practice (CNAA 1991 p.6). A second advantage is that the increasing use of competences in the assessment of, particularly, vocational education at the further education level, permits teachers to have shared in the experience they make available to their students. The clarification and making public of aims and objectives of course and how they are evidenced in assessment—though this should apply to all courses of study—is central to the notion of competence-based approaches. Tuxworth (1982) was commissioned by the Further Education Curriculum Review and Development Unit (FEU) to review competency and performance based staff development in relation to effective teaching. He describes, for example, the work of the National Center for Research in Vocational Education at the Ohio State University in Columbus, Ohio and identifies two strands of development in the States; Competency-Based Teacher Education (CBTE) and Performance-Based Teacher Education (PBTE). His introduction suggests that the Competency/Performance-Based movement which he refers to as C/PBTE to indicate the inseparability of the two systems, has made knowledge, methodology and resources for teacher education much more accessible; the technology of teaching has been separated from lengthy award bearing courses and that as a consequence, more flexibility in staff development had been provided. In the context of FE teaching where not all staff are 'trained' to teach, where there is some discontent with traditional training courses and where, he suggests, there are particular limitations to the contribution conventional award bearing courses can make in times of rapid change, there is much promise in the C/PBTE approach. His discussion is, of course, about competency-based teacher education and his definition of a competency as 'the knowledge, skills and attitudes required to perform a given task or act' (para 13 p.5) places him firmly at the performance rather than the competence end of the argument. Clearly, for in-service teachers whose essential qualifications are vocational and experience based, the opportunity for training or staff development which can be individualised, guided by feedback, systematic, modularised and which reflects exit criteria rather than entry requirements has great potential. Even within this context, however, Tuxworth warns against the assumption that the observation and assessment of successful performance implies understanding. Furthermore, since this approach suggests the possibility of a list of competencies and an associated set of performance assessment instruments and procedures without the necessary intervention of a taught course of study, the problem about the significance of what is being assessed becomes even more crucial.

Subsequent discussion of competence in the vocational field refers both to the importance of context and knowledge in relation to performance. This extends competence beyond observable performance skills but does not necessarily encompass all the elements required, for example, in the personal higher education of the undergraduate student teacher (Whitty and Willmott 1991). Can, for example, the successful learning of subject knowledge to the equivalent of a second year honours specialist student (which has been, until Circular 14/93 required by CATE criteria (DES 1989b)) be assessed by the performance of a primary student teacher in the classroom? In moving away from the simple, perhaps simplistic definitions employed in the early versions of competency and performance based teacher education we move into highly problematic areas: to what extent is it possible to judge the effect of a learning experience largely in terms of demonstrable competence? How broad a definition of competence can be employed? A narrow definition works in tension with the rationale for a liberal education; a broad based definition makes it extremely difficult to define criteria of competence in a reliable or valid way (Whitty and Willmott 1991). And if we can't define it we can't measure it. If you can measure competency (i.e. performance reflecting understanding) do you need, necessarily, to follow a course of study or can the whole burden of assuring standards be carried by the assessment process? (Whitty and Willmott 1991). Hargreaves (1989) suggested that if assessment on postgraduate certificate in education courses is to remain undifferentiated, i.e. pass/fail, what is the rationale for students remaining on a course longer than the point where they can pass? Wood and Power (1987) have a response for this in terms of 'spotty' performances but in the current political context, Hargreaves' point is a powerful one: students who have their competencies checked when they believe they are ready have the enormous incentive of the early award of QTS and professional wages. Again, the assessment process is even more crucial in the maintenance of standards.

The issue, therefore, is the resolution of the tensions between courses trying to foster learning through course curricula and learning processes as well as by the assessment of achievement (Whitty and Willmott 1991). In some ways it can be argued that an increased emphasis on assessment on competences or exit criteria within teacher education could liberate the teaching and learning processes on such courses, providing opportunities for negotiation and flexibility—key skills in the portfolio of the reflective teacher advocated by, *inter alia*, Hextall et al. (1991). However, it is more likely that teaching and learning processes will be guided by the definition of competences adopted and by the specific competences identified for assessment (Whitty and Willmott 1991). Even so, for the kind of high level skills demanded of a professional teacher it is likely that a range of assessment methods will be necessary, even in a course based almost entirely upon the achievement of workplace competences.

Although not yet developed for teacher education, principles for the assessment of Management Competence (CNAA and BTEC 1990) have been identified as follows: that assessment should meet national standards; be based upon criterion referenced processes and explicit criteria; that a wide and appropriate array of methods be employed; that work-based assessment be included; that collaborative assessment procedures be designed; that assessment be independent of the pathway to assessment and that it should be available to individual candidates as well as to a cohort of students. Similar principles could be applied to the assessment of student teachers and if we could reach agreement about definitions of competence; identification of appropriate competences; and assess them according to those principles, we could identify a similarity of standards for entry to teaching independent of the preparatory route taken. This would be a welcome contribution to teacher supply.

There remain a number of difficulties—definitions of competence which go beyond skill, for example, personal characteristics, represent particular problems in assessment, but if we maintain a definition of teacher as reflective practitioner there could be room here for self assessment (Whitty and Willmott 1991) though issues of reliability and validity become even more important. The implication is that whatever the approach taken, the assessment of competence will require inferences to be made on the basis of a range of evidence—the more specific the definition the less inferential; the less specific, the more inferential. The compromise here is the association of specific definitions with range statements which detail the different contexts within which these competences must be displayed. There remains the problem of where 'pass' occurs, whether comparative judgements can be used instead (valued added by a course of study or work experience placement perhaps?) or whether the identification of novice skills as compared with expert can give us our absolute 'pass'—norm referenced as it inevitably is. Certainly the 'consumers' of newly qualified teachers, whether defined as employers, colleagues, parents or pupils will expect the ability to do the job to be the explicit outcome of the exercise.

Competence as a red herring?

All of these problems, somewhat undermine the notion of competence assessment as clear, objective and accessible for students and employers—though the image may appear less muddy. As Norris (1991) explains, 'The requirement that competencies should be easy to understand, permit direct observation, be expressed as outcomes and be transferable from setting to setting, suggests that they are straightforward, flexible and meet national as opposed to local standards' (p.331). Similarly, the language of competence invites 'a spurious precision and elaboration in the definition of good or effective practice' (p.334). In fact, because they are tidy and precise, such definitions can distort and understate the things they attempt to represent. By describing competence in precise, transparent, observable terms, to predict the outcome of effective action, we are led to a predetermination of what constitutes good practice—perhaps the most fundamental criticism of this model of teacher education. There is a '... fundamental contradiction between the autonomy needed to act in the face of change and situational uncertainty and the predictability inherent in the specification of outcomes' (Norris p.335). Unless, Hextall et al. (1991) might argue, the outcome to be assessed is defined as flexibility of response based upon definition and redefinition of a changing situation (reflection in action using Schon's terms (1987)).

The advantages of competence-based teacher education remain to be proven while the difficulties of definition, specification and the related identification of valid and reliable criteria for assessment still dominate the early stages of this debate. The essential problem remains the assumption that assessment of knowledge or performance 'can cope with the range of context dependent and contingent nature of professional action' (p.337). 'It is not standards of performance that are required since these are beyond our capacity to specify. What is needed are standards of criticism and principles of professional judgement that can inform action in the context of uncertainty and change' (p.337). As Norris concludes, 'The trouble with competence is that it has a currency way beyond its operational and conceptual reach' (p.339).

Conclusion

In some ways, this chapter, in attempting to raise issues of assessment, is somewhat premature. Whilst definitions of competence range from the checklist of skills approach represented by C/PBTE (Tuxworth 1982) to the professional reflecting in action (Schon 1987; Elliott 1989; Hextall et al. 1991), the identification of appropriate modes of assessment is not possible. All that can be done is to identify some of the assessment problems which will emerge as a consequence of the adoption of particular definitions. This has been done *inter alia* through the arguments of Messick (1984), Wood and Power (1987) and Norris (1991) in relation to the general literature of competence in terms of educational measurement and has been related to the research on competence in teacher education/professional education by such as Elliott (1989), Whitty and Willmott (1991) and Hextall et al. (1991) which is in its infancy.

8 Mentorship and whole-school development

Brian Fidler and Norman D Lock

Introduction

We are in the process of witnessing a radical change in Initial Teacher Training in Great Britain. This is the result of both political and professional agendas. So called 'school-based' training is already in place for Secondary PGCE courses and Circular 14/93 (DFE 1993a) requires that courses for students training to be primary teachers will be in place by 1996 at the latest. The central theme of this shift in the agenda of Initial Teacher Training (ITT) is that 'schools should play a much larger part in ITT as full partners of higher education institutions' (DFE 1991 p.1). Students will be spending more time in schools and teachers will have more clearly defined roles in supporting students than they have in the past.

There has been a great deal written about the developing partnership between training institutions and the schools and the changing roles of both partners. In contrast, until very recently, an examination of the standard school management literature leaves one with the clear impression that student teachers are not a management issue. There is a dearth of information and analysis in management terms *vis-à-vis* this group. However, the increased time that students spend in school and the resulting change of role for both teachers and whole-school communities will mean that headteachers and others concerned with the leadership of schools need to consider seriously the management implications of this developed partnership. They will need to consider it in the context of a progression from initial training through induction into the early stages of further professional development for staff.

The new role of teachers in supporting students is usually referred to as 'mentoring' (Wilkin 1992; McIntyre, Hagger and Wilkin 1993). This verb is often used to describe what teachers do when they act as mentors. In this chapter the term 'mentorship' will be used to define the whole process of student learning in school because we believe that it will have an effect on the professional development of all those involved.

Mentorship

Mentorship is the term generally used for the task of the teacher-tutor in school when this goes beyond what has traditionally been associated with the role of teachers with student teachers whilst in schools. Teachers whose classes have been taken by students may have talked to students informally and offered advice, and they may have been involved in assessing student practice in association with the training institution. Mentorship requires a greater involvement of teachers with student teachers in their school and a greater involvement with tutors from the training institution in planning and delivering teacher development.

The role of the mentor towards the student teacher in school is an example of a good teacher, coach, supervisor and assessor. Part of that role will be to work with students helping them to reflect on their own practice and form their own mental frameworks to encapsulate their work.

Mentorship needs to be a whole-school issue

With their increased role in the emerging school-based models, schools need to recognise that:

- students will be spending significantly more time in school than they have in the past

- schools will have a more clearly defined and central role in student learning.

Rather than see this as a bolt-on extra for already overburdened schools, this increased involvement needs to be seen as part of a school's development plan. Indeed since the contribution of the school will be more than marginal, this involvement should be seen as part of the school's strategic plan (Fidler 1989b; Fidler et al. 1991).

Before taking on such a large commitment, the implications for teachers, parents and pupils should all be recognised and the consequences foreseen. Shaw (1992a) recommends an audit of training expertise to see who on the staff of the school has previous experience of taking part in teacher training or any similar activities. Although the worthwhileness of taking part in such an initiative may be first seen by the head and senior management team, for such an initiative to be successful, it needs the active co-operation of a large number, if not all, the teaching staff in the school, and therefore it is vital that there should be widespread consultation on the proposal and participation in the final decision to take part.

There are a number of groups who will all be affected by the decision to take a larger part in teacher training and all of these should be considered before any commitment is made.

Governors and parents

From the very beginning, the governing body will need to be included in the decision-making process concerning a school's involvement in school-based initial teacher education. This is a whole-school issue which will affect all aspects of school life.

The governing body will need to have a very clear picture of what will be involved. They will need to understand the school's commitment in terms of time and resources. They need to know who will be affected, and have an understanding of the positive and possibly negative aspects of the programme. It would be useful for a representative of the training institution as well as some representatives from schools elsewhere who are already involved to talk to the governing body.

It is likely that governors and parents would feel reassured if they knew that the school's involvement was part of the school development plan. They would need to understand that students were planned for and appropriate structures were in place to ensure minimum disruption and maximum benefit to the school. They need to understand that the *planned* presence of students will enable the school to achieve a variety of goals which will include professional staff development and enhanced learning opportunities for children.

The governors would also need to know what the school's response would be to students who are causing concern. They will need to know what arrangements have been made with the training institution as safeguards for pupils and teachers if this happens.

Parents, of course, will have more direct concerns. They may well be anxious about the direct effect of students on their children. As part of their monitoring programme, the school will be making sure that the same pupils do not have student teachers too often. It would be reassuring to parents if they were aware of such monitoring. On a more positive theme, schools should be emphasising to parents the enhanced learning opportunities created by students working with small groups and individual children. Students are not just extra pairs of hands in the classroom, but extra professional support. There is evidence that parents in primary schools are interested in what students are doing in school (Lock 1990). In that study parents commented positively on issues such as: the high level of interest shown by their children in new approaches; the quality of display work; the good relationships developed between student and children; the dedication and commitment of student teachers. Negative comments included children not being 'pushed' enough and students' lack of discipline and control. Schools will need to take the opinions of parents very seriously.

Pupils

The school will need to monitor which pupils have students working with them over a number of years. It would be unsatisfactory to pupils and unacceptable to parents and governors if some children were taught by students too frequently.

Student time in school inevitably involves some disruption to pupils. Schools will need to consider strategies to ensure that this disruption is kept to a minimum. Careful planning and maximum co-operation between the teacher and the tutor will be necessary. In many ways, schools need to be proactive here rather than reactive. Schools need to negotiate with the training institution from the outset that the focus of the time students spend in school is not simply on student performance alone, but is equally concerned with supporting pupil learning.

For the schools' part, students need to be seen as additional professional help. Through co-operative planning and teaching, mentors and students could provide significant support for pupil learning through small group and individual work. Programmes of work for such children would need to be part of the planned schedule of teacher and student. One-off, *ad hoc* arrangements negotiated at the last minute would be of limited value. Students working in consultation with tutors at the training institution and making use of the institution's comprehensive resources would undoubtedly be able to offer children a rich programme of learning.

Shaw (1992a) points out that patients are willing to accept some inconvenience when they attend teaching hospitals and hopes that teaching schools will be accepted on the same basis. However, it should be borne in mind that one of the advantages of a teaching hospital is that patients in return for being disturbed by being used for teaching purposes have the expectation that they are in particularly expert hands when they are being treated. If this analogy is carried through to schools, then teaching schools should be expected to give a standard of performance that is high and at the leading edge of developments in teaching.

Teachers

There are a whole series of questions and issues that will need to be considered by headteachers, their staffs and their governing bodies about the implications of a mentorship programme for teachers in schools.

Teachers in schools, of course, are central to any mentorship programme. Zeichner (1978), Boydell (1986), Yates (1982) and Thompson (1982) all confirm the impact that the co-operating teacher has on the attitude and behaviour of student teachers. The bulk of this research also showed that the classteacher had a much greater influence on the students' learning than the training institution supervisor. There was general recognition that classteachers were well placed to help students.

In Chapter 2 it was pointed out that students were only likely to obtain a satisfactory experience in school if they were placed in an effective school and with an effective teacher who wished to be involved and who had skills to work as a mentor with other adults. This is a formidable set of criteria and although forms of training and development for mentors should be expected, it should not be assumed, that for those staff who are unwilling or show no propensity to be good at tutoring other adults, that the limited amount of professional development which is likely to be available will be able to overcome such major obstacles.

The further requirement for courses which intend to operate on some form of reflective practitioner model is that teachers either operate in a way which is consistent with this model and can increasingly articulate their thinking or are willing and able to begin to do so. Since there is evidence that reflecting on practice is more likely to be of value to experienced practitioners than to novices (McIntyre 1993), the value for students is in beginning to acquire the skills of reflection which they will find increasingly useful throughout their career in teaching. Mentors, therefore, will need extra skills to help students to begin and extend their reflective processes.

It may be that the staff development for teachers which is involved in thinking about, reflecting on and articulating more of their practices, is a principal attraction for schools in taking part in mentoring. However, it is important to recognise the starting point for such development rather than assuming that all teachers have or could acquire all these skills.

The activities which the mentor would actually carry out each week to support the student could include, for example: watching the student teach and writing notes on the lesson observed; teaching the class for the student to observe; reading the student's school experience file; setting aside 'quality time' for reflective discussions; arranging for the student to observe other members of staff. It would be very valuable to all concerned, and would certainly help to avoid misunderstanding, if these 'agreed actions' were written into the teacher's job description and were part of the school's policy statement about its mentorship role. Similarly, there would be a need to confirm in writing a staffs' decisions about the extent to which students observe teachers other than their own mentor. There is an expectation in some models of mentorship that students observe a range of practice within the school. Teachers would need to agree that they would be willing to be involved in such a programme. There will be more about school policy statement later.

When student teachers are on their final school experience in primary schools and spend most of their time acting as teacher in sole charge of the class, thus allowing a great deal of 'free' time for their mentor, how will the mentors organise their time for maximum effect? If carefully planned in advance, there may be time for:

- their full range of mentorship responsibilities

- working with individual children and small groups

- working with other full-time colleagues in their classrooms

- working co-operatively with other colleagues, who may also be available because of the presence of students, away from the classroom in a variety of school planning activities

- undertaking activities for their own professional development.

All these activities can only happen if they are carefully planned in advance in consultation with the student and other teacher colleagues. Not to do so would mean that time would be frittered away. Teachers' time must be seen as a valuable resource which will need to be well organised.

Finally, teachers would need to be very clear about their role in the assessment of students. There is perhaps an inherent conflict between the developmental and evaluating aspects of supervision. In the USA, Blumberg (1974) questioned whether the supervisor giving guidance and help should be the one who assesses the student. It could be argued that perhaps a sensible solution would be for the teacher, student and tutor to be involved in jointly developing a formative record of the student's achievements and the setting of future goals. Whatever method is decided upon, it would be most important for the teachers acting as mentors, the professional tutors, and the students to be very clear about what happens in terms of assessment. There would need to be a clear written statement related to the competences demanded by the circulars.

Headteachers

Quite often headteachers are not directly involved with the mentorship programme. The responsibility may be delegated to the deputy head or a senior member of staff. Yet it is the headteacher who has a crucial role to play at the very start. We would argue that it is their responsibility to involve staff and governors in assessing whether or not the school is ready *at that particular time* to be involved in any mentorship programme. They should clearly not make a decision on their own without full staff and governor consultation. Mentorship will involve the whole school and will require whole-school commitment.

It may well be headteachers who express initial interest and enthusiasm in their school's involvement in mentorship because they can see the potential for staff development within such a reflective and evaluative programme. However, any strategic analysis should be undertaken in a consultative way, that is doing it with people and not to people. In this way staff are less likely to feel that they are being manipulated.

The head and senior management team may advocate the change and seek to ensure that a positive decision is made, but the proposal has to receive the backing and commitment of all of the staff who will take part.

The training course may well involve both serial and block experience in schools. Where serial experience involves school-based investigation and research, this provides an opportunity for the school to identify such projects which will be of value to the school as well as the training of student teachers. Heads will need to be proactive in identifying such areas when the detailed planning of training courses takes place if the school is also to benefit from such activities.

Headteachers may be well placed to assess how far taking part in teacher training is seen as likely to increase the school's chances of recruiting beginning teachers who have demonstrated their abilities when the supply of beginning teachers is expected to fall in the near future (Fidler 1993). Of HMI's sample of newly qualified teachers in 1992, 10 per cent of primary and 15 per cent of secondary teachers had obtained posts in schools in which they had trained (OFSTED 1993).

A school policy

Following a careful weighing up of costs and benefits for the school
and following extensive discussions with the training institution, the
school will need to decide whether a decision to take part is feasible,
suitable and acceptable (Johnson and Scholes 1993). Feasibility will
involve an assessment of whether, given other school priorities, any
commitment can be sustained in the longer term; suitability will
involve an assessment of whether for this particular school the strategic fit (taking advantage of external opportunities and internal
strengths whilst minimising external threats and internal weaknesses) is appropriate; and acceptability will involve an assessment of
whether key stakeholders, those who have an interest in the school's
success, will support the decision (Fidler 1989b, Fidler et al. 1991).

Full staff discussion on such issues would need to result in a
whole-school decision about the level of a school's involvement.
Moreover, a whole-school decision would need to be taken about the
model of mentorship that is being offered by the training institution.
If the school is not satisfied with the model being offered, the headteacher may wish to seek other alternatives, for example, the Open
University programme; approach other training institutions; set up a
local consortium of schools, buying-in training institution support
when it was thought necessary.

In any model, the headteacher would need to be satisfied that the
roles of the school and that of the training institution are clear and
unambiguous. There would need to be a form of contract between
the partners which sets out what is required by all concerned. The
'Note of Guidance from the Council for the Accreditation of Teacher
Education' on circulars 9/92 and 35/92 (CATE 1992) already sets out
the elements of such a contract between secondary schools and training institutions. Within such a contract there would need to be a
clear statement of the students' entitlement.

Although we are suggesting that there will need to be whole-
school consensus about involvement in mentorship programmes,
there may be some issues that headteachers, either alone or with
senior colleagues, would need to consider. For example:

- who on the teaching staff is best placed to be professional
  tutor or school coordinator?

- which teachers are to act as mentors? Do good teachers
  automatically make good mentors? How long should
  teachers be in post before they have anything to offer
  students? Do senior members of staff have x years
  experience, or one years' experience repeated x number of

times! Are young teachers in a better position than older members of staff to relate to young student teachers? Are headteachers aware of staff or departments who are not sympathetic to students; those who find it difficult to communicate with students; those who do not like to have their practice questioned; those who find other adults in the classroom disruptive? Do headteachers place students with staff or departments whose own professional practice is unsatisfatory?

The management issues of being involved in school-based initial teacher education are then wide-ranging, sometimes complex and will inevitably affect the whole school community. It would seem absolutely necessary, therefore, for schools to develop a written policy statement which articulates their commitment and level of involvement with initial teacher education. Such a school policy document could include:

- a statement to confirm that the school has an important and active part to play in the training of student teachers.

- a commitment from the school to organise and plan in such a way that the regular presence of students at various times in the year is acceptable and not disruptive.

- a decision about how often a school is prepared to take students, and how many students can be helped at any one time.

- a decision about who has overall responsibility for students; the professional tutor. There would need to be a clear statement about their role, responsibilities and their working relationship with other staff members.

- a clear statement about the responsibilities of the mentor.

- a clear statement about the school's role in the assessment of students.

- a commitment to involve students fully in the life of the school. Students would be encouraged to take part in staff meetings, in-service days, parent evenings, open days, field study trips and so on.

- an undertaking to allow/encourage students to see a range of staff teaching children.

- details of how the programme of monitoring and evaluation will be organised.

- an undertaking to produce and regularly update a document

for students, newly qualified teachers and newly appointed teachers which will help familiarise them with the school.

- an undertaking to ask students what they thought of the support given by the school, and how this might be improved.

We believe that such a policy statement will be most effective if the teaching staff, governors, parents and training institution tutors are involved in developing it so that each group feels that it has a level of ownership and has some commitment to making the policy work. The professional tutor would need to be on hand to ensure smooth implementation.

Managing the change

In considering the whole proposition and in preparing for it, it will be important to review previous history of taking part in teacher training. There may be a great difference between continuing and enlarging what has been done in the past and taking on a new and large commitment. If taking on the larger commitment involves an intention to encourage teachers to reflect upon and improve their practice as a result of mentoring trainees, the extent of the change required is even larger. This will not automatically come from taking part in teacher training. It may be aided by taking part in teacher training, but a separate change strategy will be needed to facilitate this change in staff attitudes and indeed the whole culture within the school. It should be remembered that any attempt to change attitudes and basic working practices is a very large change indeed and will need to be very systematic and well planned if it is to have any chance of succeeding.

Any force-field analysis (Fidler et al. 1991) which has examined driving and opposing forces of the change before it has been adopted, should subsequently be used to plan implementation. Attempts should be made to weaken opposing forces and strengthen the driving forces. A commitment chart is a useful device to examine the current stance of key staff towards the change. An assessment needs to be made of the minimum support from each of these staff for mentoring to be a success. A capability and readiness chart is also useful to assess how capable each member of staff is to take on mentoring and how ready each is to take on the responsibility. These are analytical devices (Everard and Morris 1990) to help plan how to manage each member of staff and provide the appropriate amount of training and support.

In planning the implementation of the strategy there are three key areas to consider: staffing, systems and resources (Johnson and Scholes 1993).

Staffing

There should be one principal co-ordinator of Initial Teacher Training or professional tutor in the school. This post may also involve responsibility for induction and staff development activities as a whole. This provides a person to co-ordinate all activities inside the school and also act as the first point of contact for those outside the school. Where there are separate people for initial training and post-initial development then there will be a need for co-ordination and interchange of expertise. The choice of such a principal organiser will need to weigh up the potential attractions of appointing a very senior member of staff with status and authority such as a deputy head to take on the job which will mean it is one of many of his/her activities or of choosing somebody less senior who can take this on as their principal responsibility but who may have less of a whole school view and less authority. If this really is to be part of the school's strategy then such a person should be part of the senior management team of the school. Although he or she is the principal organiser, it does not follow that he or she has to be the largest contributor, the job is organising and co-ordinating the efforts of many others.

There will be some activities that are common to all of the trainees and it makes great sense for those to be organised across the school whilst there will also be activities that involve individual teachers and subject specialists and these clearly will be carried out in each subject department in secondary schools that takes part in teacher training. Throughout it should be remembered that the individuals who take part as mentors of trainees need to be effective teachers. Whilst they may develop in the job it must be regarded as a high risk to take on somebody who is not yet an effective teacher in the hope that they might develop into one. They are likely to be extremely influential to trainees and it should be borne in mind that they are likely to be imitated by trainees.

All staff who will be involved in taking part as mentors, or co-ordinating the whole scheme, will need time to discuss and work out their role in the whole process and will need specific training and development. Whilst some training for mentors may be provided in association with other schools and the HEI, there will need to be in-school development of the mentoring group. Trainees need to be given an equivalent experience no matter what section or department of the school to which they are attached and they also should receive a co-ordinated approach both within the school and between the school and the HEI. This will take a good deal of discussion and agreement to ensure that there are common understandings of what is required. That such agreement is carried out in practice will need monitoring by the school co-ordinator. The group will also need thereafter regular times at which to get together and solve problems that have arisen.

If quite a lot of the training takes place by subject specialists in departments in secondary schools, then specific steps need to be taken to ensure that the trainee teacher acquires a balanced whole view of the role of the teacher otherwise it may well be that subject specialisms compared with pastoral activities and cross curricular activities within the school become reinforced rather than such barriers being broken down.

Of course, teachers will have to be prepared for such a mentorship role. There is clear evidence (Yates 1982; DES 1987) that many teachers are uncertain of their role in the training process. This is not the appropriate place to discuss the possible content of such a preparation programme, but it is fitting at this point to ask who will decide what should be involved in such preparation. Is this a decision taken by the training institution alone, or will teachers be in a position to identify their needs and negotiate a programme? The change in teachers' roles would need to be planned and supported within the context of a staff development programme. This underlines once again the need for the whole mentorship programme to be developed within the wider school development plan. Not to do so would make mentorship seem like a bolt-on extra where teachers make their contribution but receive little in return. Several training institutions are already accrediting teachers for their work in mentorship schemes.

A recent survey (Pomeroy 1993) showed that different teacher education institutions are approaching mentor training in different ways. The target of the training programme is the teacher in the school who is to act as mentor. Two basic types of mentorship and associated training appear to be emerging in primary schools:

Model 1a: One teacher is 'trained' at the training institution. This person becomes *the* school mentor. A variety of classteachers act as host to students, but the mentor is the named person who has responsibility for the students. They are freed from their own class if necessary (some deputies in large primary/ first/middle schools do not have classteacher responsibilities) and supervise students during school experience. In many ways they undertake a 'clone' tutor role.

Model 1b: One or two teachers are 'trained' at the training institution. They return to school and disseminate information to other colleagues who will act as mentors to students on school experience. Once again the mentors act as 'clone' tutors.

These are essentially the same model. Both are very similar in that teachers are 'trained' to carry out supervision roles. In many ways teachers take on the role of the tutor from the training institution. As a result of these teachers' duties, the training institution tutors visit the students less frequently, and in some cases not at all.

Model 2 This model is substantially different from the model above. A whole school staff undergo a mentorship preparation programme in their own school with the training institution tutor who will work with that school in an ongoing way. Mentorship involves everyone and is concerned with the professional development of students, teachers and tutors. The preparation programme helps define the role of the teacher and the tutor. It helps articulate what teachers and tutors are best placed to do to support student learning. Both teachers and tutors are seen as essential in helping students develop as active critical learners and consequently as thinking teachers. Teachers in schools are helped to share their expertise, which is implicit in their practice, with students.

In this second model the notion of partnership seems much stronger. The teachers and training institution tutor work together to provide different kinds of input to help students learn (McCulloch and Lock 1994).

Systems

The systems in the school and some policies will need amending to take account of a regular presence of trainees within the school. Their accommodation, their form of address, their receipt of mail, their access to clerical and other services, all need to be thought about and appropriate people informed.

Whilst the school will have a staff handbook either that will need amending to take account of trainee teachers or a separate handbook for trainees will need to be produced to introduce the trainees to the school and its systems. Last but not least, parents may need to be informed about the school's commitment to trainees and the repercussions of trainees taking part on a larger basis than in the past in the teaching of their children.

Resources

The training institution with which the school is working will have negotiated a sum of money which is to cover the activity of mentoring one or more trainee teachers but it may well be that the school, from its own resources, has to find some input and this will need to be justified on the basis of its contribution to staff development. Having obtained resources which are appropriate to begin the process, these need then to be allocated in terms of either time or materials.

How will the primary school, in particular, create 'quality time' to allow teachers and students to work together away from the children? In any well constructed mentorship programme there will need to be such time for teachers and students to have reflective, unhurried conversations which are not concerned with solving immediate and short-term problems. When transferred funds are made available by the training institutions, some schools may wish to buy-in occasional supply teachers to cover classes, although it could be argued that this would be yet another outside 'face' to which children would have to relate. Alternative solutions could involve using a variety of permutations of other teachers and students within the school. For example, when teacher 'A' and student 'A' are in discussion in the staffroom, teacher 'B' works with class 'A' while student 'B' teaches class 'B'. The additional benefit here is that teachers can work in other classrooms other than their own. With a carefully structured and planned approach, in a seven-week school experience period, in our example, teacher 'B' could have developed an interesting programme of work for class 'A' based on his or her own subject specialism.

Evaluation

Any mentorship programme within a school would, of course, need to be monitored and evaluated. The professional tutor would seem to be in the best position to undertake this task. This teacher would need to monitor the performances of the student teachers, the teachers acting as mentors, the pupils and the tutor from the training institution. Procedures and contingency plans would need to be in place well in advance of the school experience period. At key points in the on-going programme there would need to be an evaluation of the effects on the whole school, individual teachers and on pupils and their work. Such evaluations would need to be shared with the whole school and the tutor from the training institution, allowing effective policy and practice to be identified and disseminated and any difficulties to be addressed.

Conclusion

Any decision to take part in school-based training is very far-reaching and needs consideration from a number of perspectives. There are complex issues which affect the whole school community. These need debate and much detailed planning. However, for a lively school there is much to be gained from taking part in the challenging and complex activity of preparing future teachers.

9 Integrating mentorship into higher education institutions: implementation issues

Myra McCulloch

Introduction

This chapter seeks to explore some of the issues involved in the management of change during implementation of mentorship schemes in higher education institutions. The implications for schools, of changing roles and responsibilities through the increased policy emphasis on school-based training have been discussed in some detail here and elsewhere (McIntyre et al. 1993; Shaw 1992a; Wilkin 1992). What is equally significant but has been explored less frequently is the enormous change to be accommodated within higher education not, relatively straightforwardly, only through the management of resource reduction as significant sums are transferred from HEI to the schools for their additional contribution to training, but also through the re-conceptualisation of the role of the university tutor in Initial Teacher Education. The experience of the developing primary mentorship scheme at the University of Reading will be used to illustrate some of the points raised. This scheme is the subject of a research project (McCulloch M and Lock N D) funded by the university's Research Endowment Trust Fund, for which support we are most grateful.

The policy thrust discussed in Chapter 1 could be seen to represent the separation in initial training of the professional, best done in schools by teachers and the academic, best done in universities by lecturers. This simplistic representation fails to take into account the relationship between theory and practice developed over the past twenty years in teacher education and the necessity for practice in schools to be critically appraised whilst student-teachers are learning their roles—as students and teachers. Carr (1993) reflects that, in his view 'No good reason has yet been offered . . . to support the general presumption that increased school experience will, of itself, improve the quality of teaching in schools' (p.17). McIntyre (1993) writes of the 'primitive view' of teacher education which has dominated the policy arena and advocates a view of theoretical knowledge which 'should be treated . . . as tentative, inadequate and constantly to be questioned and, where appropriate, falsified: but it should also be knowledge which we offer them because we believe it to be of practical value to them as teachers' (p.41).

This combination and constant interaction of knowledge acquisition and craft skill development marks a view of student-teacher learning which is rooted in process and content and which requires a transformed approach to teaching and learning in schools and universities throughout all elements of professional preparation. Watching experienced teacher performance is not enough to understand the elaborate nature of teacher competence (see Chapter 7). Similarly, discussions of theoretical insights into teaching and learning processes can only be integrated into a student-teacher's developing professional repertoire by explicit incorporation into the planning, implementation and evaluation of classroom strategies. Successful integration implies that 'different kinds of relevant knowledge, but equally important kinds of knowledge, should be accessed from university and school sources' (McIntyre 1993 p.42). This has profound implications for the preparation in partnership of school teachers for their transformed role (discussed by Fidler and Lock in this volume). For as Mintzberg (1983) suggests in his discussion of the Professional Bureaucracy 'there is no control of the work aside from that by the profession itself, no way to correct deficiencies that the professionals themselves choose to overlook' (p.206).

Integration has equally great significance when considering the transformed role of the university tutor. The tentative nature of knowledge, the assumption of difference and dissent rather than conformity and consensus, for example, imply a new meaning for the term 'expert'. Expertise becomes the source from which students are helped to challenge what is and to seek what might be in all aspects of their professional development. This is very different from the apprenticeship model where students are gradually

inducted into some consensual view of what teaching is. It is also a
very challenging model of the role of the tutor and it should not be
assumed that the management of this change will be unproblematic.

Simply to adopt a series of principles or intentions as policy is not
enough. The formulation of policy should ensure, as part of its
development, that the policy *can* be implemented (Elmore 1989).
This implies not merely a technical solution to a particular problem—mapping out a pattern of teaching and learning for school-
based work in partnership, for example, but also a structural or
organisational dimension. Can the internal systems respond to the
needs of the policy change both instrumentally and affectively? Will
the members of the organisation seek to make it happen? Structures,
patterns of organisational behaviour and attitudes at key points are
likely to be highly significant.

Elmore suggests that there is not much help in understanding
these issues to be gained from the implementation research. '. . .
when we look to the most influential implementation studies for
guidance about how to anticipate implementation problems, we find
advice that is desultory and strategically vague' (p.224). He suggests
that this is due to a reluctance on the part of policy analysts to take
the risk of suggesting a 'logically ordered sequence of questions that
policy makers can ask, prior to making a policy decision, that will
provide prescription for action' (p.244). Essentially, he argues, this
is because the conventional mode of policy formulation and implementation starts from the wrong end. It begins with an objective
or statement of the policy maker's intent; it then elaborates a series
of steps which are presumed to ensure the fulfilment of that objective
and it states the outcome against which success or failure can be
measured.

Unfortunately, this 'top down' model makes a number of assumptions which lead to suggestions about its effectiveness. The
most significant is that the policy makers have correctly identified
and defined the problem and that they control the various processes
which affect implementation—organisational, political and technological. This is what Elmore (p.246) refers to as the 'noble lie' of
conventional public administration and policy analysis. What administrators and analysts find difficult to accept is that most of what
happens in the implementation process *cannot* be explained by the
intentions and instructions of the policy makers. Elmore suggests a
strategy of backward mapping which he identifies as having the
potential to take this into account; it does not exclude the interest of
policy makers in the implementation process, but suggests that they
start with the problem and work backwards to policy formulation.
Elmore asks the question, what is the behaviour that generates the
need for a policy? In order to make a difference, what are the

organisational operations and resulting set of effects or outcomes to be achieved? Can the relevant agency of implementation (school, university, department, etc) respond—does it have the ability to do so? does it have the resources or what will be required to supplement resources? What policy can be formulated to direct resources at the organisational units likely to have the greatest effect on the change in hand?

In some ways backward mapping allows contingency to be introduced. Success in implementation can be seen as conditional in that it is 'Predicated on an estimate of the limited ability of actors at one level of the implementation process to influence the behaviour of actors at other levels and on the limited ability of publication organisations as a whole to influence private behaviour' (Elmore p.247). It also challenges the assumption of hierarchical authority as an indicator of potential to achieve effective change. '. . . the closer one is to the source of the problem, the greater is one's ability to influence it . . .' (p.247). This permits the assumption of more democratic, reciprocal power structures within organisations or alternatively it allows ways of explaining the reinterpretation or subversion of policy intentions at the grass roots level.

The use of this kind of implementation strategy, therefore, permits the analysis of '*how to use the structure and process of organisations to elaborate, specify and define polices*' (p.249). Such analyses (Bolam 1984) should recognise that change has a number of key features—it is located in a particular social context; it is a dynamic process, not an event; it is an interactive process such that participants are changed by their very participation in it. Change cannot be reified and the process of implementation is both crucial and difficult to pin down. Given these features, Bolam identifies key characteristics of successful innovations—relevant, offering explicit benefit, simple and flexible, congruent with the values of the target group and feasible. The implementation of successful innovations tend to occur in contexts where the change agent is perceived favourably by members of the target user group; the organisation is receptive to change; staff morale is high; there is active support from within the hierarchy of authority; there is general support from the local education authority (or other relevant policy making body); there is commitment from teachers (or other actors) and the organisation and its members should be adaptive.

This analysis makes the process of policy formulation and implementation seem rather neat and tidy. Bolam (1984 p.40) reminds us not to put too much faith in rationality. 'This ignores the common sense and research evidence that many, and indeed probably most, teachers, like other professionals, generally, for example, don't use systematic planning techniques and methods, don't read research reports, don't like to use systematic self-appraisal methods and prefer to behave intuitively.' The preferred approach of most education professionals is 'muddling through' (p.41).

Pressman and Wildavsky's work (1979) provides further support for the more contingent understanding of successful policy implementation. They report that in their study of the Oakland project 'Chains of unanticipated decision points, requiring numerous clearances by different actors, had provided the occasions for frustrating delays' (p.69). 'Then as latent conflicts become manifest, the original agreements have to be renegotiated and a new and possibly more antagonistic situation emerges' (p.92). 'As one delay succeeded another, the major individual participants changed and so did the understanding they had with one another. Agreements were reached, eroded and remade' (p.92). Thus they suggest a series of characteristics which impede successful policy implementation. These include incompatible and simultaneous commitments; competition between projects for most favoured treatment; dependence on differentially committed partners; competing opinions and procedures and, finally, lack of power (pp.99–100). 'We conclude that the probability of agreement by every participant on each decision point must be exceedingly high for there to be any chance at all that a program will be brought to completion' (p.107).

Fullan (Fullan et al. 1991) gives further evidence of the characteristics of successful educational change. He also emphasises the complexity of the process and the anxiety and fear of loss which make change both painful and much resisted. 'Real change ... represents a serious personal and collective experience characterised by ambivalence and uncertainty' (p.32). Thus, 'shared meaning', 'shared cognition', or 'interactive professionalism', ... goes a long way in making significant change a reality' (p.46). Another dimension stressed by Fullan is the time span for successful policy change in implementation—three to five years for moderate change; five to ten years for major restructuring. The elapse of time allows for three broad phases in the change process; the initiation, mobilisation or adoption phase; the implementation or initial use and the continuation, incorporation, routinisation or institutionalisation phase. Outcomes can then be evaluated in relation not only to changes in behaviour but also to the structural impact on an organisation. The initiation or first phase takes place when planning shows evidence of Relevance (practicality and need), Readiness (Capacity and Need) and Resource availability (p.63). Fullan also reminds us of the importance of external factors in affecting the context of change. However reluctant the target group in the local context may be to accept either the definition of the problem according to policy makers or policy analysts, the different levels of power must be recognised.

Nevertheless 'No matter how much advance staff development occurs, it is when people actually try to implement new approaches and reforms that they have the most specific concerns and doubts' (p.85). Powerful forces may initiate particular forms of change, but they rely for their implementation on those closest to the problem—so policies may be carried out which have theoretically had their finding and support withdrawn or policies may exist in theory but, in practice, not be implemented.

Fullan makes a further series of points which argue for a democratic approach to policy formulation and implementation. For example, do not assume that yours is the right version of change or that change can occur without conflict and disagreement. Do not assume people will accept the need for change or that they will be consistent in their response. Do not assume that the most precise and detailed analysis will result in a clear proposal for action.

The arguments for a contingent understanding of change become more powerful and relate closely to the work of, for example, Weick (1976) and Orton and Weick (1990) which develops a model of loose coupling to explain 'the simultaneous existence of rationality and indeterminacy' (Orton and Weick p.204). The indeterminancy is, at least in part, due to individuals' bounded rationality—no one ever has the full picture; people move in and out of discussions at different times; different constituencies become involved and thus when decisions do get taken they are partial, contingent and often ambiguous. This raises another possibility in the response to change. 'People at all levels of the educational system have power—power most often used *not* to do things' (Fullan 1991 p.347).

Features, intended and unintended of the initiation and early implementation stages in mentorship developing at Reading

Chin and Benne (1976) identify three types of strategies for change; empirical rational, normative re-educative and power based. Each reflects a model of the organisation of the social world: the first assuming that human action is rational and that rational self-interest is the key driving force once it is revealed to us; the second that rationality and self-interest are constrained within patterns of socio-cultural norms which guide action; the third that the application of power ensures compliance. None of these models reflects the degree of irrationality incorporated into social organisation at a time of rapid change. Wallace (1992) identifies three approaches; the rationalistic, which may be appropriate at a time of stability where the environment is relatively predictable; a 'satisfying' approach which seeks a satisfactory rather than a 'best' solution and the Garbage Can model (outlined by March and Olsen in 1979) which reflects a denial of rationality in decision-making. In this latter model ambiguity is the norm. Goals are unclear, poorly defined and inconsistent; there is a limited understanding of the organisation; there is a variable participation in decision making and individuals who do participate move in and out of the process thus reinforcing their partial knowledge of the system. Problems, solutions, participants and choice opportunities intermingle fortuitously producing idiosyncratic and contingent decisions.

This model, stressing ambiguity, uncertainty and variability closely reflects the features of implementation of change in higher education over the past few years. In many ways, it can be argued, following Weick (1976) and Orton and Weick (1990) it is this loose coupling of parts of the organisation from the central core that permit a period during which cultural change can take place. In the political (in the sense of the internal micropolitical) context much can be achieved without conflict where lines of negotiation are somewhat blurred and no group seeks to impose an explicit and potentially unpopular solution.

In its early stages, work on mentorship at Reading was centred on a research group which focussed on the research agenda, the ideas, the evidence, the arguments. It was clear that its role was to generate 'leadership' in the field of mentorship. 'Leaders set the course for the organisation; managers make sure the course is followed. Leaders make strategic plans; managers design operational systems for carrying out the plans. Leaders stimulate and inspire; managers use their interpersonal influence and authority to translate that energy into productive work' (Louis and Miles 1990 pp.19–20). Unfortunately the 'leaders' on the research front do not necessarily, or even ordinarily, represent the same group as those who manage the institution and its daily teaching role. This can add a layer of problems to the process of change management. To the intended consequences of the initiation process: promoting the challenge of change, disseminating the ownership of change, managing resistance to change and so on are added a series of unintended complications where distinctive cultures attach themselves to the old and the new and grow to represent competing political groups. 'Balkanisation' takes place where 'a culture made up of separate and sometimes competing groups, jockeying for position and supremacy like loosely connected, independent city states' (Fullan and Hargreaves 1992 p.71) undermines whatever collegial feeling has been generated.

Exacerbating these internal political tensions has been the deteriorating political context within which teacher education is operating. The transfer of resources to schools without additional funding being made available to the system necessarily implies a vulnerability of jobs in higher education. Bowe and Ball (1992) recognise this as a key flaw in managing change—the often unexplained assumption that one fact of change can be addressed in isolation along with a neglect of institutional history suggesting that life begins with the moment of innovation. Typically, they argue, the management of change has been and is a history of conflict. It is rarely the technical and consensual process portrayed in some organisational theory. '. . . complexity is exacerbated by the incoherence of change itself and the fundamental contradictions, or incompatibilities embedded in the policy . . .' (p.146). 'This places a strong pressure on . . . managers to "manage", i.e. to recreate and rebuild, reconstruct and redefine the institutional context and the places of those within it as well as those significant others who stand "outside"' (p.156). Mentorship developments must, in this context, seek to offer the ideas and new meaning which will permit such explicit management strategies to respond to external pressures on initial teacher education and to internal uncertainties about the value in which individuals and their skills are held. It implies an understanding of change as a political and cultural activity (House 1981).

Handling the problems of change

Knowing the theory of how to handle change does not necessarily make the change process straightforward. Bennett et al. (1992) argue that '. . . the best way of thinking about how to deal with change is by being eclectic' (p.4). '. . . pragmatism informed by a clear sense of meanings and values, which recogises the role of "theory" in developing a sense of good practice' (p.4). Further, 'The basis for deciding on a particular course of action is not the rational evaluation of data but a combination of data, gossip, best guessing and hunch' (p.7). The case of mentorship, driven by a research agenda seeking systematically to investigate a strategic implementation programme is problematic in the context of this view of the non-rationality of implementing change. It reveals numerous difficulties in trying to achieve not just competing but contradictory aims. Is it doomed to failure or is there potential for dialogue between the research and the implementation where each feeds on the other? 'Political models see all decisions as being actual or potential occasions for conflict, and therefore expect constant negotiation to take place routinely in order to achieve anything' (p.9).

This political notion of space for manoeuvre, negotiation and the inevitability and desirability of conflict as a creative force, is useful in understanding what actually happens when change is implemented. Bowe and Ball (1992), using examples taken from school-based change, argue that instead of policy taking 'the form of something that is done to teachers rather than with them, still less by them' (Fullan and Hargreaves p.27), Bowe and Ball argue that 'Here the silent voices are heard, but they speak either as theoretically overdetermined mouthpieces of a world beyond their control or as potentially free and autonomous resisters or subverters of the status quo' (Bowe and Ball 1992 p.6). Policy in implementation, becomes potentially something to be interpreted, contextualised; something from which new meanings and interpretations can be generated. Policy becomes a discourse where possibilities and impossibilities are tied to knowledge and practice, to values and their 'authoritative allocations' (p.13). Bowe and Ball argue that there are three primary policy contexts within which these processes take place; the context of influence (at the policy initiation level—for example in ITE, the introduction of school-based Initial Teacher Education by the DFE), the context of policy text production (the representation of policy—through the work, for example, of the Council for the Accreditation of Teacher Education which has sought to define the parameters within which partnerships with schools shall be developed) and the context of practice where 'policy writers cannot control the meanings of their texts' (p.22); here is where the creative strategies of the institution can recreate change according to shared meanings reflecting internal cultures.

The two pilot studies currently being carried out on primary mentorship in Reading, involve whole-school development in preparation for mentorship in partnership with the university. They confirm the view that although firmly rooted in the same, explicit principles and systematically planned to implement the same strategy, each of the two schools has taken the research project and interpreted and reconstructed it in its own context and to suit its own purposes. The role of the university tutor as facilitator in this context permits the reinterpretation to take the form of a dialogue rather than encouraging co-option of the innovation (i.e. beyond ownership) by the school. For 'It takes a fortunate combination of the right factors—a critical mass—to support and guide the process of re-learning, which respects the maintenance needs of individuals and groups and at the same time facilitates, stimulates, and prods people to change through a process of incremental and decremental fits and starts on the way to institutionalising (or, if appropriate, rejecting) the change in question' (Fullan 1992a p.128).

Fullan (1992a) conceptualises such change in terms of three key elements: the characteristics of the innovation or change project, the roles of the local community which form the context for the change and the external or political framework within which change is taking place. Those committed to a rationalistic approach will find this challenging for he suggests that understanding the need for change may not emerge as far as the participants are concerned until the change project is under way (the Garbage Can analysis would confirm this in terms of a solution looking for a problem); any clarity about goals and means is often false clarity (we know exactly what we are doing but we are mistaken); that small, incremental changes are achievable, give immediate feedback but make no substantial change whilst large scale, high risk projects are much more prone to failure on a grand scale but paradoxically achieve more. Though, 'The answer seems to be to break complex changes into components and implement them in a divisible and/or incremental manner' (p.114). In terms of the local and wider political context the more support, particularly demonstrated through action, the better, though again 'When it comes to institutionalisation the larger the external resource support, the less likely the effort will be continued after external funds terminate, because the district will not be able to afford to incorporate the costs into its regular budget' (Yin et al. 1977 p.16).

Despite the ambiguities, the contradictions and the unforeseen circumstances—or at least unintended if not unforeseen—Fullan (Fullan et al. 1991) identifies several key themes which contribute to successful policy initiation, mobilization or adoption (Phase I) leading to Phase II, implementation or initial use and, if successful, Phase III, the continuation, incorporation, routinisation or institutionalisation process. The themes, developed in the work of Louis and Miles (1990), are features of an adaptive model of change (p.123) which is vision-driven, guided by judgements not rules, accountability based, team focused, network based (semi-autonomous or 'loosely coupled' (Weick 1976; Orton and Weick 1990), multi-specialised and involved with the whole person.

Again, taking the example of work done with teachers, Fullan and Hargreaves (1992) reinforce the point. 'Teacher change and teacher development . . . is very much bound up with the development of the total person' (p.15). 'What matters here is *not just whether the particular model is valid or not, but how it connects to a teacher's overall sense of purpose in the particular situation in which he or she is working*' (p.31). Furthermore, 'total teachers . . . are most likely to emerge, develop and prosper in total schools, in schools which value, develop and support the judgement and expertise of all their teachers in the common quest for improvement' (p.35). The same, it is argued here, applies to university tutors.

Thus, in Reading, the mentorship project seeks to endorse this view, firstly, through its strategy of initiating a faculty wide policy on mentorship which permeates all Initial Teacher Education programmes from the nursery phase to further education training and through the four-year undergraduate BA(Ed) programme as well as the one-year postgraduate certificate courses. Secondly, the project adopts a whole-school approach whereby the commitment to partnership in teacher education is not with individual academic departments or headteachers but with whole schools who, after full discussion, agree to incorporate this model of student teacher learning into their School Development Plan. In this way commitment to the values as well as the processes of change is sought. But this strategy also emphasises the scale of the endeavour; change of this magnitude and of this kind (challenging meaning) carries with it a high risk of failure.

The power of the status quo

Huberman (1992) describes Fullan's work 'to enumerate and intertwine the multiple levels at which the change process operates' (p.3) and notes the depth of feeling engendered by change; 'informants feel that implementation had been mismanaged—some even talked about "betrayal"' (p.5). This comes of there being 'too-many-moving-parts' (p.6) in the process and thus the greater chance of internal turbulence. The feeling of betrayal is compounded by the innovators who see resistance as foot dragging and by treating it in this way so create it. We try, with unproven practices, 'to change people's professional lives, while at the same time changing their stable working arrangements' (p.7). It is not surprising, in these circumstances, that 'what constitutes school "improvement" for some means "rubbish" for others, at least initially' (p.16). Besides which, the critics may have a point, as Fullan (Fullan et al. 1991) reminds us.

Rudduck (1991) suggests that 'In our efforts at change I think we have underestimated the power of the existing culture of the school and classroom to accommodate, absorb or expel innovations that are at odds with the dominant structures and values that hold habit in place' (p.28). In other words it is not just the political but the cultural context which is crucial in change. We need '... to see change not simply as a technical problem but as a cultural problem that requires attention to context and to the creation of shared meaning within working groups'(p.30). The creation of shared meaning is crucial; not just the management but the meaning of change. What is needed is teachers who are 'those who recognise a potentially creative dissonance that they are prepared to confront and deal with' (p.91).

The change process is a mysteriously complex and paradoxical affair. Wallace (1992) offers a list of factors affecting planning: the multiplicity of goals, unpredictable crises, inability to predict policy shifts, difficulty in securing resources and so on. But even taking all these into account, planning may not triumph over adversity. Fullan (Fullan et al. 1991) offers some advice. For example, do not assume that your version of change is the only one; allow individuals to make their own meanings and to own the change; welcome conflict and disagreement as creative features of change; assume that pressure will be needed to move things forward and this will take time and still not affect all people; do not jump to conclusions about the possible reasons for lack of implementation; assume you need to plan on the basis of all these uncertainties but that no amount of knowledge will make it totally clear what action should be taken. The culture of the organisation is the real focus for change and this, of course, is the most difficult thing to affect (pp.105–107). 'The aspiration towards a shared commitment to change is ambitious in the sense that the habits and structures that hold traditional values in place are not easily dismantled' (Rudduck 1991 p.129). This is further exacerbated when, for example, in this mentorship scheme the attempt is being made to transform the culture of the faculty *and* the cultures of the schools with which we work. 'The difficulty in the relationship between external and internal groups are (*sic*) central to the problem and process of meaning. Not only is meaning hard to come by when two different worlds have limited interaction, but misinterpretation, attribution of motives, feelings of being misunderstood and disillusionment on both sides are almost guaranteed' (Fullan 1992a p.119).

Conclusion

Wallace (1992) warns that in the current turbulent context a balance has to be achieved between planning for maintenance and development. Anticipatory features such as information deficit, haphazard processes such as intuition and guesswork and the need to proceed in an ad hoc manner all contribute to the difficulty of finding this balance. At the same time we must beware of the belief that activity represents progress. Fullan (1991) warns that 'most changes, even the big restructuring ones, have a pacifier effect because they give the appearance that something substantial is happening when it is not' (p.352). The dangers of attempting a great deal, risking failure yet achieving nothing in the context of a very resistant status quo are clear. What seems to be the central message and one to which the Reading mentorship group returns after identifying it as an issue two years ago (McCulloch 1993b) is that size and scale make the transformatory endeavour both worthwhile and seemingly impossible.

10 Improving initial teacher training?

Brian Fidler and Myra McCulloch

Introduction

The purpose of reform must always be to improve a situation defined as being less than the best we can imagine. It is hard to envisage any teacher educator unable to think of ways in which our current activities could be improved. Nevertheless it is important to ask of the current reforms, whose definition of improvement is to hold sway, whose vision of the future is to inform change and if there is any dispute about what constitutes 'improvement' how these differences might be resolved? In this debate there are a number of opinions which might be sought. What are to be the processes of consultation, discussion and resolution?

For the purposes of anlaysis and recommendations it is valuable to disaggregate two inter-related concepts. One is the process by which change is accomplished and the other is the nature of the change itself. It is quite possible to conceive of a good change badly implemented but less likely, but quite possible, to go through appropriate processes but to decide on a less than successful change. A change process which follows sound principles is more likely both to decide upon an appropriate change and to implement it successfully.

Managing change and improvement

Managerial principles

Whole system change is not brought about successfully by statute alone. In Chin and Benne's (1976) terms this is the power-coercive approach. This assumes that individuals act like automatons and do as they are told. Simple changes can be accomplished in this way if they are adequately policed but more complex change which requires individuals to interpret and make judgements cannot be so simply achieved. More is required.

The positive way forward is to articulate and share a vision of an improved future. It is not enough just to identify deficiencies in the present situation, an alternative has to be proposed. This is the least that should be done. Then the participants actually have some idea of the proposed outcome. This approach relies upon the assumption that the justification of the deficiencies is accepted, that it is possible to achieve the improvement and that the participants are willing and able to play their part. This is the normative-re-educative approach of Chin and Benne which uses persuasion and the affective dimension of human behaviour.

To increase the chances that the contributions of those involved in the change will be forthcoming there needs to be active participation in discussions about the desirability and feasibility of the vision and the creation of practical plans to achieve the vision. This requires time and expertise. The vision must be tested for its desirability—does it represent an effective solution to present problems and future needs? Moreover, is the vision feasible? Given foreseeable constraints, can the vision be implemented? What are the crucial factors which underlie its success? If individuals understand the answers to these questions and are at the very least persuaded of the worthwhileness of the proposals, they are in a position to have an overview of the changes and be able to make appropriate decisions rather than blindly follow a narrow and inadequate understanding of what is required.

To inform both the vision and the planning to achieve the vision there needs to be a rational assessment of the present and its shortcomings. This is the empirical-rational component of Chin and Benne's approaches to change. What is the evidence on the present state of trained teachers? The HMI/OFSTED reports on the teaching skills of new teachers in schools have become increasingly positive since the first report in 1982. This is especially true when the other two factors which make for a successful start to a teaching career are taken into account—appropriate placement and induction. The first report made clear that a sizeable proportion of the unsuccessful teaching was due to teachers being appointed to jobs for which they were untrained and unsuited. Appropriate training and placement still require a suitable professional induction and support in the first teaching post. High quality teaching in the first post relies on appropriateness of all three of these:

- education and training
- placement in post
- induction and support.

There is a very good case supported by the evidence for identifying the real problem with teacher training as not being with the immediate performance of teachers after training but with the longer term growth of the professional during his or her career. The need is to view and plan for training, induction and further professional development as a whole. Training has to provide the suitable launch pad for this longer term endeavour as well as producing teachers with appropriate practical skills on completion of training.

The Government's approach

The publication of the HMI report on school-based training (HMI 1991) only weeks before the speech at the North of England Conference by the then Secretary of State (Clarke 1992) which forecast Circular 9/92 (DFE 1992) gives pause for thought. The views expressed in the HMI report were closely though critically related to the aims and intentions of practice in the teacher education establishments. The announcement by Kenneth Clarke assumed no existing commitment on the part of teacher education to provide relevant training with effective and substantial experience of the workplace, the school. The gap of understanding between the views of Her Majesty's Inspectorate and Her Majesty's Government is a pale shadow of the gap between Her Majesty's Government and what has come pejoratively to be called the education establishment. Are you in it? Are we? Whether or not we see ourselves as members, the flavour of the debate is not that of collaborating professionals but of a political agenda distinct from and, in principle opposed to, the views of those in the profession.

Broadfoot (1986) asked the question whether the line could be held in maintaining a consensual framework in education policy making. It seems not. The agenda for reform of teacher training, therefore, is clearly seen to be in the control of the Department for Education and to be resistant to the consultatory opinions offered by the profession (whether in the schools or th universities). In this context it is ha.d to imagine a posiuon where all reforms will be unproblematically adopted by teacher educators. Where there is no permanent forum for sharing collaborative planning criteria and no notice is taken when consultative procedures are adopted (the Blue Book on the proposed Teacher Training Agency (DFE 1993b) is the best recent example of this). It cannot be a surprise when teacher education institutions are suspicious about and reluctant to adopt the agenda, open and hidden.

The point seems to be made that the government is not convinced by the evidence presented to it by its own arm of inspection. Sadly one can go further. The introductory paragraphs of the

Reform of Initial Teacher Training (The Blue Book) actually misrepresent the evidence presented by HMI to make it appear as if standards are in question whereas in fact the report is considerably more positive than negative. Newsam (1993) is scathing in his critique of the integrity of a government department which can initiate a consultation process on the basis of misrepresentation, particularly when it very soon became clear that the consultation was a sham. The debate in the House of Lords on the Education Bill which emerged from this 'consultation' (House of Lords 1993) showed overwhelming, almost unanimous opposition to the proposals presented there. Despite the depth and political breadth of the opposition, including some of its traditionally loyal supporters, the Government was able to persuade its traditional supporters to vote in sufficient numbers to secure the passage of the amended Bill to the House of Commons where it is currently (at the time of writing) under discussion. The support for the Lords reflected throughout the higher education system was somewhat muted by their last minute surrender to political expediency though the effectiveness of the lobby provided by the Teacher Alliance (including the Teacher Unions and The Universities Council for the Education of Teachers (UCET)) in close liaison with the Committee of Vice-Chancellors and Principals (CVCP) showed that at least there is life still in the system and that close alliances can be very effective when mutual interests are at stake. The raw use of political power can only be resisted when those who are part of that system choose to stand up and be counted for just a moment longer.

The underlying problem continues to be that the agenda for improvement adopted by the profession is quite different from the agenda of reform proposed by the government. Although the same words are being used, quite different things are meant and each side is persuaded of the lack of integrity of the other.

What needs to be done

At present we lack even a vehicle for any discussion of the vision of the future or the difficulties involved in its realisation. There is no GTC and no longer an ACSET forum. CATE which did not meet these needs is going to be disbanded. Any idea that a small hand-picked TTA board could fulfil this function is risible. An *ad hoc* representative group of teachers, teacher trainers, HMI, DFE and LEAs as in Northern Ireland is an obvious short-term measure, though there appears to be some consideration now of a Royal College of Teachers with a rather more limited role than the profession would wish.

The changes themselves

The proposals

Turning from the process to the vision—what is the vision and is it desirable and feasible?

We consider only those proposals affecting main-stream Initial Teacher Training. For all the reasons articulated in the discussion of the need for partnerships between schools and HEIs, schemes which are school-centred without an adequate HE component appear to be heading for the craft model of teaching which we have no hesitation in condemning as inappropriate for the long-term success of children's learning in school.

What are the key areas for discussion? The model of teacher education made explicit in the circulars; the nature of partnership between schools and higher education institutions in terms of what each is best placed to do; the transfer of resources and the implications of this for both the division of labour in initial teacher training and the infrastructure of advanced studies and research in education; the relationship between initial preparation, induction and continuing professional development; the protection of the entitlements of pupils in a system which is being asked to take on increasing responsibility for student-teachers; the effective management of quality assurance in a dispersed system and the implications of failure in relation to the university's role in validation; the preparation of teachers for the future not simply teachers adequately trained to cope with the present. Alongside this is the political notion of a market or near market in teacher education which seeks to establish numerous routes of entry into teaching without necessarily establishing convincing means by which their equivalence in terms of competence or quality can be assured.

An assessment of the proposals

Is the vision for mainstream teacher training also of a teaching force with improved practical skills in the short term at the expense of longer term professional knowledge, understanding and attitudes? Is the view of teaching for which trainees are preparing that of a craft? If so, more on-the-job training under the tuition of good crafts people would be what is required.

But this would be counter to developments in education in almost all other advanced nations and counter to developments in other advanced occupations. In these other spheres people with theoretical knowledge and frameworks for thinking which provide flexible foundations for development and improvement throughout their careers are what are required. A secure preparation for an unchanging task is an increasing anachronism. The craft metaphor is the wrong vision.

The desirable vision is of the professional.

The model of teacher education assumed by the circulars is a competence-based model based upon output criteria which seek to identify the minimum level of skills and knowledge acceptable in a newly qualified teacher. The difficulty in defining what competence means and therefore what might be appropriate competences for a beginning teacher has been rehearsed elsewhere. The fundamental question is whether those who adopt a model of teacher preparation rooted in the notion of the reflective practitioner can see room for this to be encompassed within a competence-based model. Can competence be understood in such a way as to accommodate the necessary skills related features which will serve to convince the most sceptical of critics that teacher education is doing an effective job and at the same time, accommodate the notion of a teacher as a thinking professional who conforms to Schon's (1987) notion of the reflective practitioner? If, as Hextall et al. (1991) argue, reflection can be conceived as a competence, there may be room for agreement.

The nature of the partnership between teacher educators in the university and schools sharing a view of what each is best placed to do depends upon the achievement of a shared model of teacher preparation which recognises the distinct and valuable contribution each party has to make to the education of intending teachers. This implies time having been spent in debate, argument and reflection for it is neither self evident nor rooted in research evidence that teachers and tutors will have a shareable view of what constitutes the most effective form of teacher preparation. This uncertainty is exacerbated by each party finding some difficulty in making explicit exactly what it is they *do* know and being able to place this in relation to what others know of teaching which might be useful and relevant to novices. McIntyre (1993) is quite clear about the need for all contributors to teacher education to concern themselves with the process and content of learning about becoming and being a teacher and ensuring that their distinctive vision is included in initial teacher preparation.

The transfer of resources from higher education to schools is an area fraught with difficulty. In the first place the policy states that only the additional work created by the two Circulars (9/92 and 14/93) will be resourced with new (i.e. transferred) funds. Schools (and LEAs) have been unable to identify the existing budget lines which are supposed to cover their current contribution to ITT. Furthermore the transfer assumes a simplistic model of training where it is easy to determine who does what and where; the schools do the pedagogy and the universities do the subjects. This is not a model of preparation which finds favour with either teachers, tutors or students. The teachers have a role to play in what have traditionally (but mistakenly) been thought of as theory courses and the tutors have a role to play in pedagogy—not so much the 'this is what to do here' but the 'why is this done here and how might it be done otherwise, elsewhere?' The Oxford model (Benton 1990) shows convincingly how difficult and how important it is, for training to be effective, that each party to the partnership has a clear, explicit and considered position on what it is they know and can do in the training of student teachers. In this way the appropriate resources can be transferred with all parties having the confidence that the money is being well spent in the most effective programme of training.

The impact on this transfer of resources for other parts of the university department's role in teacher education has yet to be experienced but must give rise to considerable concern. A wide provision of in-service and higher degree supervision can only be sustained on the foundation of a broadly based programme of initial teacher education. The wide range of staff needed to give proper expertise, in depth, to the issues which must be confronted in teacher education requires an infrastructure which begins to be affected as resources are transferred out of the departments. The research carried out by HMI (1991) and the NFER (Stradling et al. 1991) confirms that the school-based model of teacher education is more expensive than those models currently in operation. Yet the current proposals suggest that the system can accomplish all the changes imposed by the criteria with reduced rather than enhanced funding. The reluctance of the government to accept evidence gathered by the most independent of researchers must imply a reluctance to accept any evidence which might cause its agenda to be interrupted, even though that evidence implies that standards (which the government is avowedly committed to raising) will clearly be undermined.

The relationship between initial training, induction and continuing professional development is another area where deeds would speak louder than words. The development of a scheme which seeks to identify beginning, early and later competences for teachers and which seeks to locate these in a framework where schools and higher education institutions contribute each in their own way to the parts they are best placed to provide, has been conducted in Northern Ireland (DENI 1993a) but not in relation to England, Wales and Scotland. This is clearly one way forward which would give all parties greater confidence in the desire of the policy makers to ensure a comprehensive and high quality system of professional development rather than a cheap and not very cheerful one.

The resource issue is one which relates not only to the lifelong learning conception of professional development for teachers but also to the initial learning entitlement of all pupils under the provision of the 1988 Education Reform Act (House of Commons 1988). If teacher education is to become more school-based and if teacher education is to be under resourced, the necessary implication is that the school budget intended to fund the education of pupils through the National Curriculum may be raided to make good the needs of the students in training. Schools with a strong commitment to planned expenditure may be able to resist the insidious drain on their resources; others, less well managed and protected may not see the extent to which their prime purpose is being challenged to subsidise an underfunded higher education system.

Quality is a crucial aspect of all of this. The key aim of reform, must be to do things better. At present the quality assurance procedures in place in universities are scrutinised systematically and regularly by the internal procedures of the institution, monitored by the Higher Education Quality Council. Quality assessment is carried out by the Higher Education Funding Councils in liaison with OFSTED. OFSTED assures us that the criteria for assessment of entirely school-based schemes of teacher education will be exactly the same as those for university based courses. How can this be so when so much of the quality of HE based courses is rooted in the nature and quality of the partnership arrangements? Can it be said that one side of the partnership is seen as so much more important than the other that free standing courses are seen to offer benefits beyond criticism? This must be subject to the most rigorous monitoring if any confidence at all is to be placed in some of the alternative routes into teaching proposed by the government and if they are to gain any kind of credibility. The difficulties implied, for each higher education institution, of monitoring, with a reduced staffing base, the extensive and extended school-based work role of all partner schools, are great enough. If university authorities are unconvinced of the possibility of monitoring and maintaining standards in such a dispersed system and begin to consider the withdrawal of validation, the fear that policy will de-intellectualize the system (Kelly 1993) will multiply.

The final fear in relation to the current proposals for reform is that the teachers trained under these criteria will be suited only for the present climate. The range of intellectual skills and knowledge which would equip them for a lifelong, varied, demanding and unpredictable career in a changing and developing education system having been replaced by a series of competences related to what is demanded by the current state of the art, (teaching the National Curriculum) implies an inability to move beyond the status quo. The apprenticeship model can provide only some of the characteristics required of the professional teacher and they tend to be those reflecting what is, not what might be.

But in a system which admires diversity this is seen as no bad thing. Alternative routes provide alternative kinds of teacher. Unfortunately they do not provide equivalent kinds of teacher but this is not a debate which attracts much support. Where the competences to be used to assess students for the award of Qualified Teacher Status are different depending upon the route from which one enters teaching, questions have to be asked about which list actually constitutes the basic minimum. Does our QTS mean the same as yours? If not, what then? After years spent in pursuit of a graduate profession and all the status, confidence and discipline associated with that notion, it is hard to see these fundamental principles undermined by default.

What should be done

Preparation for partnership is the real challenge. Having agreed upon the desirable end product of training, how to achieve this is problematic. A more integrated partnership between schools and teachers and HEIs and tutors is almost certainly part of the process of improving the preparation of these new professionals. More time in school does not follow as a requirement and there is evidence that the depth of the partnership depends on other factors than length of time in school (Furlong et al. 1988; HMI 1991; Miles et al. 1993).

The real difficulties for this transition involve

- resources in *addition* to those currently available

- the need to involve *sufficient* good schools and teachers

- how to develop HEI tutors and school mentors to play their *respective parts* in this new enterprise.

Concluding themes

What other themes have emerged from this volume? A significant development seems to be the more democratic nature of the relationships between higher education and schools. This must be seen as essential if authentic partnerships are to be sustained. Nevertheless the process of establishing partnerships of this kind is not without its difficulties. Each partner has to experience a transformation of role in which new demands and expectations are being made, some of which are enormously testing in the context where many staff believe firmly in the traditional role models, well established over many years. A transitional period during which strategic plans are made for the long-term fulfilment of true partnerships would seem to be necessary so that the interests and aspirations of all parties, including our student teachers can be guaranteed. This might also ease some of the problems related to the transfer of funds, not the simple matter many in Government appear to think it.

The difficulties of establishing authentic partnerships are, however, seen by all the contributors to this volume to be worth the effort. Each institutions represented here had gone some way along the road to collaborative not simply co-operative planning and delivery of initial course preparation. This would seem to confirm the view that were open and trusting means of sharing professional planning available between all interested parties the deep suspicions and hostility which mar our education service at present might be ameliorated.

There does seem also to be a site of debate on competence which will need to be further explored. The majority of teacher education courses seek to establish the teacher as a reflective practitioner. That is, someone who is operating much beyond the technician level. That is not to debase the technical expertise undoubtedly needed by teachers; it is simply to argue that they need to be something more than this. To be able to use their technical skills to best effect by making judgements about the educational progress of the whole child. The kinds of concerns which are close to the heart of the current Secretary of State (John Patten), values, consideration, commitment to the community, have actually never disappeared from our schools or from teacher education but the time available and the prevailing ideology of subject centredness paradoxically undermine what must be at the heart of the educated person. The autonomous professional is a person who can thrive in the challenging, developing framework of our education system. The ability to be self-critical and to develop skills for sustainable personal and professional development has to be central to this concept; the notion of competence which we employ must be able to accommodate this. Furthermore, this seems to be the kind of professional that student teachers aspire to be. What evidence is there that alternative routes into teaching will be attractive to intending teachers?

Another theme which has emerged from this collection is the notion of learning on many sites in many inter-related and complementary ways. None of the courses discussed here conceives of the school as a place where one kind of learning happens and the university as the place where another kind takes place. Schools and universities exist in communities; students, tutors, teachers and their pupils belong to those communities in a variety of ways. All of these contexts inform what and how we learn and, indeed, provide us with the secure base from which we can speculate about alternatives. The richness of the educational experience is enhanced by these complementary (and sometimes contradictory) experiences and this should not be undermined by simplistic notions of the division of labour between higher education and schools in the particular example of student-teacher learning. Indeed the fear is explicitly expressed in this collection that a policy intended to foster partnerships, actually, by virtue of its reluctance to embrace complexity, is serving to undermine the quality of existing partnerships.

Partnership is also confirmed in these accounts as a whole school issue. Students are being prepared not only as subject or classroom teachers but also as members of the school staff who have responsibilities to their colleagues, to governors, to parents and to the community and society. Achieving a partnership scheme which takes all this as given is not easy but the aspiration must be central to future developments.

It is the aspirations expressed here and the means by which a variety of teacher educators are seeking to achieve them that inform the question with which we began. Will the changes currently proposed actually improve teacher training? Certainly there is evidence of much improvement in the provision of initial training in the past ten years. There is also evidence, not least in the accounts presented here, of the constructive, creative, innovative ways in which improvement of student-teacher learning has been sought. What difference to this learning will the proposed establishment of the Teacher Training Agency make? What improvement will the arbitrary increase in the time spent in school rather than in higher education make? What effect will the creation of a three-year, six-subject degree have? What will be the long-term impact on initial, in-service and research degree provision? What is the intention informing these proposals and why have they been pursued with such remorselessness despite the almost unanimous opposition of all concerned? Why is consultation no longer a process in which educators feel any confidence?

The answer to these questions depends, of course, on where one is standing at the time. Indeed, unless equipped with a crystal ball it would be impossible to answer the majority of them. It is sad, however, to see the extent of the breakdown between the policy makers and the professional educators and if there is a conclusion to be drawn from the experience of the past few years it is that the best possible provision will only be guaranteed by the re-establishment of a forum within which, if not a consensus, at least principles and a code of practice can be agreed for the promotion of efficient, effective and imaginative teacher education. Improving Teacher Training? Yes please, let's do that.

References

Archer M S (1985) Educational Politics: a Model for their Analysis in McNay I and Ozga J (eds) *Policy Making in Education: The Breakdown of Consensus*, Oxford: Pergamon Press, pp.39–64

Ball S J (1987) *The Micro-Politics of the School: Towards a Theory of School Organisation*, London: Methuen

Barber M (1993) The truth about partnership, *Journal of Education for Teaching*, 19(3), 255–262

Bennett N and Carre C (eds) (1993) *Learning to Teach*, London: Routledge

Bennett N, Crawford M and Riches C (eds) (1992) *Managing Change in Education: Individual and Organizational Perspectives*, London: Paul Chapman Publishing

Benton P (ed) (1990) *The Oxford Internship Scheme: Integration and Partnership in Initial Teacher Education*, London: Calouste Gulbenkian Foundation

Blumberg A (1974) *Supervisors and Teachers: A Private Cold War*, Berkeley, CA: McCutchan

Bolam R (1984) Recent research on the dissemination and implementation of educational innovations in Campbell G (ed) *Health Education and Youth: a Review of Research and Developments*, Lewes: Falmer Press, pp.247–254

Bowe R and Ball S J with Anne Gold (1992) *Reforming Education and Changing Schools*, London: Routledge

Boydell D (1986) Issues in Teaching Practice Supervision Research: a review of the literature. Paper presented at the conference on 'Teaching Practice Supervision in Primary Schools', College of St. Paul & St. Mary 10 July 1986, Cheltenham: College of St. Paul & St. Mary

Broadfoot P (1986) Power relations and English education: the changing role of central government, *Journal of Education Policy*, 1(1), 53–62

Bush T (1986) *Theories of Educational Management*, London: Harper and Row

Calderhead J and Gates P (eds) (1993) *Conceptualizing Reflection on Teacher Development*, London: Falmer Press

Carr D (1993) Guidelines for teacher training: the competency model, *Scottish Educational Review*, 25(1), 17–25

Chin R and Benne K D (1976) General Strategies for Effecting Change in Human Systems in Bennis W G, Benne K D, Chin R and Corey K E (3rd edn) *The Planning of Change*, New York: Holt Rinehart and Winston, pp.22–45

Clarke K (1992) Speech for the North of England Conference, London: DES

Council for National Academic Awards (1992) *Competence Based Approaches to Teacher Education: Viewpoints and Issues*, CNAA Project Report 33, London: CNAA

Council for National Academic awards (CNAA) and Business and Technician Education Council (BTEC) (1990) *The Assessment of Management Competence: Guidelines*, London: CNAA/BTEC

Council for the Accreditation of Teacher Education (CATE) (1992) A Note of Guidance, London: DFE

Crozier G, Menter I and Pollard D A (1990) Changing Partnership in Booth M,

Furlong J and Wilkin M (eds), *Partnership in Initial Teacher Training*, London: Cassell, pp.44–56

Darling-Hammond L, Wise A E and Pease S R (1983) Teacher evaluation in the organisational context: a review of the literature, *Review of Educational Research*, 53(3), 285–328

Dearing R (1993), *The National Curriculum and its Assessment. An Interim Report*, York: National Curriculum Council and School Examinations and Assessment Council

Dearing R (1994) *The National Curriculum and its Assessment: Final Report*, London: SCAA

Department of Education Northern Ireland (DENI) (1993a) *Review of Initial Teacher Training (ITT) in Northern Ireland: Report of Three Working Groups on:—Competences (Working Group I)—Courses, Cooperation and ITT Structures (Working Group II)—Coordination of ITT, Induction and In-Service Training (Working Group III)*, Belfast: DENI

Department of Education Northern Ireland (DENI) (1993b) *Review of Initial Teacher Training (ITT) in Northern Ireland: Report of the Development Group (Working Group IV)*, Belfast: DENI

Department for Education (DFE) (1992) *Initial Teacher Training (Secondary Phase)*. Circular 9/92 and 35/92, London: DFE

Department for Education (DFE) (1993a) *The Initial Training of Primary School Teachers: New Criteria for Courses (Circular 14/93)*, London: DFE

Department for Education (DFE) (1993b) *The Government's Proposals for the Reform of Initial Teacher Training*, London: DFE

Department of Education and Science (DES) (1977) *Education in Schools, A Consultative Document*, London: HMSO

Department of Education and Science (DES) (1983a) *Teaching in Schools: The Content of Initial Training*, London: HMSO

Department of Education and Science (DES) (1983b) *Teaching Quality* (Cmnd 883), London: HMSO

Department of Education and Science (DES) (1984), *Initial Teacher Training: Approval of Courses (Circular 3/84)*, London: DES

Department of Education and Science (DES) (1987) *Quality in Schools: the Initial Training of Teachers*, London: HMSO

Department of Education and Science (DES) (1989a) *The Education (teachers) Regulations (Circular 18/89)*, London: DES

Department of Education and Science (DES) (1989b) *Initial Teacher Training: Approval of Courses (Circular 24/89)*, London: DES

Department of Education and Science (DES) (1989c) *Standards in Education 1987–88: Report of the Senior Chief Inspector (SCI)*, London: DES

Department of Education and Science (DES) (1992a) DES News Press Release 158/92. *Patten announces Expansion of School-Based Teacher Training*, London: DES

Department of Education and Science (DES) (1992b), *Curriculum Organisation and Classroom Practice in Primary Schools: a Discussion Paper (The Alexander, Rose and Woodhead Report)*, London: DES

Dinham S M and Stritter F T (1986) Research on Professional Education, in Wittrock M C (ed), *Handbook of Research on Teaching* (3rd end), New York: Macmillan Publishing Co, pp.952–970

Edwards A (1993) *Teacher Education: Partnership in Pedagogy*, British Educational Research Association (BERA) Annual Conference Paper, Liverpool, unpublished

Elliott J (1989) Appraisal of Performance or Appraisal of Persons in Simons H and Elliott J (eds) *Rethinking Appraisal and Assessment*, Milton Keynes: Open University Press, pp.80–99

Elliott J (1990). But do they understand?, *Education*, 20 April 1990, 393–394.

Elmore R F (1989) Backward Mapping: Implementation Research and Policy Decisions in Moon B, Murphy P and Raynor J (eds) *Policies for the Curriculum* London: Hodder and Stoughton, pp.244–256

Esp D (1993) *Competences for School Managers*, London: Kogan Page

Everard B and Morris G (1990) *Effective School Management*, London: Paul Chapman Publishing

Everton T and Impey G (1989) *IT—INSET: Partnership in Training: The Leicester-shire Experience*, London: David Fulton Publishers

Fidler B (1989a) Background to the Education Reform Act in Fidler B and Bowles G (eds) *Effective Local Management of Schools; A Strategic Approach*, Harlow: Long-man

Fidler B (1989b) Strategic Management in Schools in Fidler B and Bowles G (eds) *Effective Local Management of Schools; A Strategic Approach*, Harlow: Longman

Fidler B (1992) Job Descriptions and Organisation Structure in Fidler B and Cooper R (eds) *Staff Appraisal and Staff Management in Schools and Colleges*, Harlow: Longman

Fidler B (1993) Balancing the Supply and Demand for School Teachers, in Fidler B et al. (eds), *The Supply and Recruitment of School Teachers*, Harlow: Longman

Fidler B and Bowles G with Hart J (1991) *ELMS Workbook: Planning Your School's Strategy*, Harlow: Longman

Fidler B, Fugl B and Esp D (1993) *The Supply and Recruitment of School Teachers*, Harlow: Longman

Fitch T (1994) The economics of mentoring, *Mentoring*, 1(3), 29–33

Fullan M G (1992a) Causes/Processes of Implementation and Continuation in Bennett N, Crawford M and Riches C (eds) (1992) *Managing Change in Education: Individual and Organizational Perspectives*, London: Paul Chapman Publishing, pp.109–131

Fullan M G (1992b) *Successful School Improvement*, Buckingham: Open University Press

Fullan M G and Hargreaves A (1992) *What's Worth Fighting for in Your School: Working Together for Improvement*, Buckingham: Open University Press

Fullan M G with Stiegelbauer S (1991) *The New Meaning of Educational Change*, London: Cassell

Furlong V J, Hirst P H, Pocklington K and Miles S (1988) *Initial Teacher Training and the Role of the School*, Milton Keynes: Open University Press

Gage N L (1978) *The Scientific Basis of the Art of Teaching*, New York: Teachers College Press

Glass G V (1978) Standards and criteria, *Journal of Educational Measurement*, 15(4), 237–261

Glazer N (1974) The schools of the minor professions, *Minerva*, XII(3), 346–364

Handal G and Lauvas P (1987) *Promoting Reflective Teaching: Supervision in Action*, Milton Keynes: SRHE and Open University Press

Hannon P and Welsh J (1993) Bringing parents into initial teacher education in the context of a school partnership, *Educational Review*, 45(3), 279–291

Hargreaves D (1989) PGCE assessment fails the test, *Times Education Supplement*, 3 November 1989, 20

Harrison J K and Pritchard K J (1992) What do schools expect of our trainee science teachers in the teaching of broad and balanced science at Key Stage 4?', *Education in Science*, No. 149, 9–11

Her Majesty's Inspectorate (HMI) (1988) *The New Teacher in School: A Survey by HM Inspectors in England and Wales, 1987*, London: HMSO

Her Majesty's Inspectorate (HMI) (1991) *School-based Initial Teacher Training in England and Wales: A Report by HM Inspectorate*, London: HMSO

Hextall I, Lawn M, Menter I, Sidgwick S and Walker S (1991) *Imaginative Projects; Arguments for a New Teacher Education*, London: Goldsmiths' College

House of Commons (1988) Education Reform Act: Chapter 40, London: HMSO

House of Lords (1993) Education Bill, London, HMSO

House E R (1981) Three Perspectives on Innovation: Technological, Political, and Cultural in Lehming R and Kane M *Improving Schools: Using what we know*. Beverley Hills, CA: Sage

Huberman M (1992) Critical Introduction in Fullan MG *Successful School Improvement*, Buckingham: Open University Press

Hughes M (1985) Leadership in Professionally Staffed Organisations in Hughes M, Ribbins P and Thomas H (eds), *Managing Education: The System and the Institution*, London: Cassell, pp.262–290

Interactive Skills Ltd (1992) *An Interim Functional Analysis of four major areas of applied psychology*. Henley on Thames. British Psychological Society (Project commissioned for the BPS and funded by the Employment Department)

Jarvis P (1983) *Professional Education*, London: Croom Helm

Johnson G and Scholes K (1993) *Exploring Corporate Strategy* (3rd edn), London: Prentice Hall International

Johnson T J (1972) *Professions and Power*, London: Macmillan

Jones L V (1971) The Nature of Measurement in Thorndike R L (ed) *Educational Measurement* (2nd end), Washington, DC: American Council on Education, pp.335–355

Kelly A V (1993) Education as a field of study in a university: challenge, critique, dialogue, debate, *Journal of Education for Teaching*, 19(2), 125–139

Lawlor S (1990) *Teachers Mistaught: Training in Theories or Education in Subjects?*, London: Centre for Policy Studies

Leicestershire Partnership Scheme for Initial Teacher Training (1993) *Science Handbook*, Leicester: University of Leicester School of Education

Lock N D (1990) Student Teachers in School. Unpublished MSc dissertation, University of Reading

Louis K S and Miles M B (1990) *Improving the Urban High School: What Works and Why*, New York: Teachers College Press

Luft J (1961) The Johari Window, *Human Relations Training News*, 5(1), 6–7

Lunt N, McKenzie P and Powell L (1993) 'The right track: teacher training and the new right: change and review, *Educational Studies*, 19(2), 143–161

March J G and Olsen V P (1979) *Ambiguity and Choice in Organisations* (2nd edn), Oslo: Universtets for laget

McCulloch M (1993a) Trends in Initial Teacher Preparation in Fidler B, Fugl B and Esp D (eds) *The Supply and Recruitment of School Teachers*, Harlow: Longman

McCulloch M (1993b) What is involved in good school-based teacher education?, *Journal of Teacher Development*, 2(1), 39–45

McCulloch M and Lock N D (1994) Mentorship developments in the primary phase of initial teacher education at the University of Reading, *Mentoring*, 1(3), 21–28

McIntyre D (1993) Theory, Theorizing and Reflection in Calderhead J and Gates P (eds) *Conceptualizing Reflection on Teacher Development*, London: Falmer Press

McIntyre D, Hagger H and Wilkin M (eds) (1993) *Mentoring*, London: Kogan Page

McKenna G (1990) What's in it for the mentors? Lessons from teacher induction, *Mentoring International*, 4(1), 2–10

McNamara D (1991) Subject knowledge and its applications: problems and possibilities for teacher educators, *Journal of Education For Teaching*, 17(2), 113–128

Menter I (1989) Teaching practice stasis: racism, sexism and school experience in initial teacher education, *British Journal of Sociology of Education*, 10(4), 459–473

Messick S (1984) The psychology of educational measurement, *Journal of Educational Measurement*, 21(3), 215–237

Miles S, Barrett E, Barton L, Furlong J, Galvin C and Whitty G (1993). Initial teacher education in England and Wales: a topography, *Research Papers in Education Policy and Practice*, 8(3), 275–304

Mintzberg H (1983) *Structure in Fives: Designing Effective Organisations*, Englewood Cliffs, NJ: Prentice-Hall

Mitchell D E and Kerchner C T (1983) Labor Relatioms and Teacher Policy, in Shulman L S and Sykes G (eds), *Handbook of Teaching and Policy*, New York, NY: Longman, pp.214–238

Morrison K (1989) Training teachers for primary schools: the question of subject study, *Journal of Education for Teaching*, 15(2), 97–111

National Curriculum Council (1993). *Associates' Briefing: Initial Teacher Training* (Summer edition)

Newsam P (1992) Profits from partnership, *Times Educational Supplement*, 13 November 1992, 19

Newsam P (1993) Pestered with a popinjay, *Times Educational Supplement*, 17 September 1993, p.20

Norris N (1991) The Trouble with competence, *Cambridge Journal of Education*, 21(3), 331–341

Office for Standards in Education (OFSTED) (1993), *The New Teacher in School, a Survey by HM Inspectors in England and Wales, 1992*, London: HMSO

Orton J D and Weick K E (1990) Loosely coupled systems: a reconceptualisation, *Academy of Management Review*, 15(2), 203–223

Patten J (1993) Speech to the Higher Education Funding Council, March 1993, London: DFE

Pomeroy R (1993) Mentorship training: the current picture, *Mentoring*, 1(2), 9–14

Pressman J L and Wildavsky A (1979) *Implementation* (2nd edn Expanded), Berkeley, CA: University of California Press

Rudduck J (1991) *Innovation and Change*, Buckingham: Open University Press

Schein E H (1972) *Professional Education: Some New Directions*, New York: McGraw-Hill

Schon D A (1983) *The Reflective Practitioner: How Professionals Think in Action*, London: Maurice Temple Smith

Schon D A (1987) *Educating the Reflective Practitioner: Towards a New Design for Teaching and Learning in the Professions*, San Francisco, CA: Jossey Bass

Shaw R (1992a) *Teacher Training in Secondary Schools*, London: Kogan Page

Shaw R (1992b) School-based training: the view from the schools. Cambridge Journal of Education, 22(3), 363–375

Stewart R (1991) Management Development for Today and Tomorrow in Ribbins P, Glatter R, Simkins T and Watson L (eds) *Developing Educational Leaders*, Harlow: Longman

Stradling R with Jamison J and Morris M (1991) *Evaluation of the Articled Teachers Scheme*, Slough: NFER

Taylor W (1990) The Control of Teacher Education: The Council for the Accreditation of Teacher Education in Graves N J (ed) *Initial Teacher Education Policies and Progress*, London: Kogan Page

The Scottish Office, Education Department (1992) *Initial Teacher Training: Draft Revised Guidelines for Teacher Training Courses*, Edinburgh: The Scottish Office

Thompson L L (1982) Faculty and student perceptions of early field experiences. Paper presented at the Annual Meeting of the American Educational Research Association, New York 1982

Tuxworth E N (1982) *Competency in Teaching*, London: Further Education Curriculum Review and Development Unit (FEU)

University of the West of England (UWE) (1993) *The Initial Teaching of Primary School Teachers: New Criteria for Course Approval: Response from the Faculty of Eduction*, Bristol: UWE

Van Manen M (1977) Linking ways of knowing with ways of being practical, *Curriculum Inquiry*, 6(3), 205–228

Vygotsky L S (1962) *Thought and Language*, New York: Wiley

Wallace M (1992) Flexible Planning: a Key to the Management of Multiple Innovations in Bennett N, Crawford M and Riches C (eds) *Managing Change in Education: Individual and Organizational Persepctives*, London: Paul Chapman Publishing, pp.151–165

Walsh K (1987) The Politics of Teacher Appraisal in Lawn M & Grace G (eds), *Teachers: The Culture and Politics of Work*, Lewes: Falmer Press, pp.147–167

Waterson A (1994) The 1991 evaluation of National Curriculum assessment in science at Key Stage 1, *Education Section Review*, 18(1), 20–26

Weick K E (1976) Education organizations as loosely coupled systems, *Administrative Science Quarterly*, 21, 1–19

Whitehead J and Menter I (1993) Partnership in Initial Teacher Training: Redefining Professionalism?, British Educational Research Association (BERA) Annual Conference Paper, Liverpool, unpublished

Whitty G and Willmott E (1991) Competence-based teacher education: approaches and issues, *Cambridge Journal of Education*, 21(3), 309–318

Wilkin M (ed) (1992) *Mentoring in Schools*, London: Kogan Page

Williams A (1993) Teacher perceptions of their needs as mentors in the context of developing school-based initial teacher education, *British Educational Research Journal*, 19(4), 407–420

Williams E A, Butt G and Soares A (1992) Student perceptions of a secondary postgraduate certificate in education course, *Journal of Education for Teaching*, 18(3), 297–309

Wood D (1988) *How Children Think & Learn*, Oxford: Blackwell

Wood R and Power C (1987) Aspects of the competence-performance distinction: educational, psychological and measurement issues, *Journal of Curriculum Studies*, 19(5), 409–424

Wright N (1993) Counting the cost of students in the classroom, *Education*, 27 August, 156–157

Yates J W (1993) Student-teaching: results of a recent survey, *Educational Research*, 24(3), 212–215

Yin R K, Herald K and Vogel M (1977) *Tinkering with the System: Technological Innovations in State and Local Services*, Lexington MA: Lexington Books

Zeichner K (1978) The student teaching experience, *Action in Teacher Education*, 1, 58–62

Zeichner K M and Liston D P (1987) Teaching student teachers to reflect, *Harvard Educational Review*, 57(1), 23–48

Index